Anselm & Becket

Two Canterbury Saints' Lives
by JOHN OF SALISBURY

John of Salisbury (d. 1180), a scholar, author and diplomat, was numbered among the *eruditi*, the learned clerks in service to Theobald and to Thomas Becket, successive archbishops of Canterbury. Indeed, John was a member of Becket's household and present in the cathedral when the archbishop's infamous murder occurred, albeit from a rather ignominious position, concealed in the shadows of the darkening church. Within two years of that fateful event, John composed a brief *Life* of his friend, the martyr. This would be his second biography of a saint. The first was written at the behest of Archbishop Thomas Becket early in 1163 for inclusion in the dossier presented to Pope Alexander III at the Council of Tours petitioning the pope to canonize Anselm (1033–1109), a former archbishop of Canterbury. Although neither of these biographies has secured the universal acclaim that modern scholars have bestowed on John of Salisbury's other writings, both certainly warrant scholarly attention.

This translation of the *Lives of Anselm and Becket* finally makes available in English all the known writings of John of Salisbury. These two works are his only contributions to the genres of biography and hagiography. In them we see how this notable Christian humanist employed his considerable rhetorical skills to create lasting literary memorials to figures of great importance in English ecclesiastical history. His profound concern for the freedom of the Church, his loathing of tyrants and tyrannical behavior, his affection for the classics and Sacred Scripture, are themes woven into his accounts of the lives and activities of two archbishops of Canterbury who endured indignity and exile for the sake of Church liberty. One authored renowned treatises in philosophy and theology; the other suffered a cruel martyrdom and secured undying fame. Both are canonized saints.

MEDIAEVAL SOURCES IN TRANSLATION 46

Anselm & Becket

Two Canterbury Saints' Lives,
by John of Salisbury

Translated by

RONALD E. PEPIN

PONTIFICAL INSTITUTE OF MEDIAEVAL STUDIES

LIBRARY AND ARCHIVES CANADA CATALOGUING IN PUBLICATION

John, of Salisbury, Bishop of Chartres, d. 1180
    Anselm & Becket : two Canterbury saints' lives / by John of Salisbury ;
translated by Ronald E. Pepin.

(Mediaeval sources in translation, ISSN 0316-0874 ; 46)
Translation of Vita sancti Anselmi and Vita sancti Thomae.
Includes bibliographical references and index.
ISBN 978-0-88844-298-7

    1. Anselm, Saint, Archbishop of Canterbury, 1033–1109. 2. Thomas, à
Becket, Saint, 1118?–1170. 3. Catholic Church – England – Canterbury –
Bishops – Biography. 4. Christian saints – England – Canterbury – Biography.
I. Pepin, Ronald E. II. Pontifical Institute of Mediaeval Studies III. Title.
IV. Series: Mediaeval sources in translation ; 46

BR754.A56J6413 2009   270.092'242234   C2009-900223-X

Contents

This book is dedicated to

Fr. Hugh Feiss, OSB

and the Benedictine Monks

of Ascension Priory,

Jerome, Idaho

Preface

John of Salisbury (d. 1180), a scholar, author and diplomat, was numbered among the *eruditi*, the learned clerks in service to Theobald and to Thomas Becket, successive archbishops of Canterbury. Indeed, John was a member of Becket's household and present in the cathedral when the archbishop's infamous murder occurred, albeit from a rather ignominious position, concealed in the shadows of the darkening church. Within two years of that fateful event, John composed a brief Life of his friend, the martyr. This would be his second biography of a saint. The first was written at the behest of Archbishop Thomas Becket early in 1163. It was intended for inclusion in the dossier presented to Pope Alexander III at the Council of Tours in May of that year petitioning the pope to canonize Anselm (1033–1109), a former archbishop of Canterbury. Although neither of these biographies has secured the universal acclaim that modern scholars have bestowed on John of Salisbury's other writings, both certainly warrant scholarly attention.[1]

This translation of the *Lives of Anselm and Becket* finally makes available in English all the known writings of John of Salisbury. These two works are his only contributions to the genres of biography and hagiography. In them we see how this notable Christian humanist employed his considerable rhetorical skills to create lasting literary memorials to figures of great importance in English ecclesiastical history. His profound concern for the freedom of the Church, his loathing of tyrants and tyrannical behavior,

---

1. In fact, the two *Lives* are more often labeled "disappointing" and "inadequate," due mainly to their brevity. For examples of this view, see Michael Staunton, *The Lives of Thomas Becket* (Manchester, 2001) 7; Frank Barlow, *Thomas Becket* (Berkeley, 1990) 3; Cary J. Nederman, *John of Salisbury* (Tempe, 2005) 80.

his affection for the classics and Sacred Scripture, are themes woven into his accounts of the lives and activities of two archbishops of Canterbury who endured indignity and exile for the sake of Church liberty. One authored renowned treatises in philosophy and theology; the other suffered a cruel martyrdom and secured undying fame. Both are canonized saints.

* * *

Friends of John of Salisbury, and my own, have encouraged me to translate these Lives. I am glad to acknowledge the gracious reception and guidance that my proposal received from James P. Carley and Fred Unwalla at PIMS. I am grateful to the anonymous readers for their candid, insightful suggestions; to Jean Hoff for her meticulous, masterful editing of the texts; and to Matthew P. Pepin for his computer expertise. Finally, for many pleasant, instructive discussions of medieval monasticism and English saints, I thank Ellen Martin and Fr. Hugh Feiss, OSB.

Introduction

Life and Works

The main outlines of John of Salisbury's life and career have now been well established, and his writings have received ample scholarly attention in the last half-century.[1] He was born at Old Sarum near modern Salisbury around 1118. Nothing is known with certainty of his earliest education, except that as a boy he was tutored by a priest who unsuccessfully attempted to employ him in the magical art of crystal-gazing.[2] In 1136 John went to study in Paris, where he remained for some twelve years. A lengthy autobiographical passage in his *Metalogicon* (2.10) details his studies and describes his masters there, including Abelard and Gilbert of Poitiers.[3] In 1148, supported by a letter of recommendation from Bernard of Clairvaux, John entered the service of Archbishop Theobald at Canterbury. His duties involved him in frequent and sometimes extended travel on the continent and in England. By 1159 he could write that he had crossed the Alps no fewer than ten times, in addition to trips to Apulia and throughout Gaul.[4]

In the curia at Canterbury, John met and became fast friends with the archdeacon, Thomas Becket. Although the view that they

---

1. Cary J. Nederman's recent *John of Salisbury* contains a fine, concise study of John's life and career. An important collection of scholarly papers on various aspects of John's life and work is found in Michael Wilks, ed., *The World of John of Salisbury* (Oxford, 1984).

2. *Policraticus*, 2.28.

3. See K.S.B. Keats-Rohan, "John of Salisbury and Education in Twelfth-Century Paris from the Account of His *Metalogicon*," *History of Universities* 6 (1986) 1–45, and Keats-Rohan, "The Chronology of John of Salisbury's Studies in France: A Reading of 'Metalogicon' II.10," *Studi Medievali*, 3rd ser. 28 (1987) 193–203.

4. *Metalogicon*, 3.prologue.

were close friends has been challenged,[5] at the very least John was loyal to Becket and remained in his service when the latter succeeded Theobald as archbishop in 1162. He actively supported Becket throughout the lengthy dispute with King Henry II. In fact, John himself had aroused the indignation of the king in 1156, and in 1163 or early 1164 he preceded Becket in exile. He soon took up residence in Rheims with his old friend Peter of Celle, abbot of Saint Rémi, and stayed there for the most part until his return to England in November 1170. John was present in Canterbury Cathedral when Becket was assassinated on 29 December 1170, and within a few weeks he recorded the events there in a famous letter (*Ex insperato*) to John, bishop of Poitiers.

John of Salisbury was appointed treasurer of Exeter in 1173. In August 1176 he became bishop of Chartres and died there in October 1180. He was buried in a chapel of Jehosaphat Abbey in Leves, near Chartres, where his stone sarcophagus may still be viewed, although his remains were transferred in 1905 to a vault of Saint Piat's chapel behind the cathedral. The necrology of Chartres reported his passing as follows:

> ... a man of great piety, illuminated by rays of all knowledge, in word, life and morals a pastor amiable to all, unmerciful to himself alone. [6]

Centuries later, John Henry Cardinal Newman (1801–1890) would list John of Salisbury among English saints and scholars "recommended to our religious memory by their fame, learning or the benefits they have conferred on posterity."[7]

---

5. Barlow, *Thomas Becket*, 20. See also John McLoughlin, "The Language of Persecution: John of Salisbury and the Early Phase of the Becket Dispute (1163–1166) in *Studies in Church History* 21 (1984) 73–87, and Anne J. Duggan, "John of Salisbury and Thomas Becket" in *The World of John of Salisbury*, ed. Wilks, 427–438, reprinted in *Thomas Becket: Friends, Networks, Texts and Cult* (Aldershot, 2007).

6. "... vir magne religionis, tociusque scientie radiis illustratus, verbo, vita, moribus pastor omnibus amabilis, soli sibi nimis crudelis." E. de Lépinois and Lucien Merlet, "Necrologium Ecclesiae Beatae Mariae Carnotensis," *Cartulaire de Notre-Dame de Chartres* (Chartres, 1862–1865) 3: 202.

7. John Henry Newman, *Apologia pro vita sua*, ed. David J. DeLaura (New York, 1968) 247.

Although surely composed in hours stolen from the press of administrative affairs, John of Salisbury's writings have been highly praised by modern scholars, and John himself has been acclaimed as "the most learned man of his day" and "one of the foremost intellectuals of his era."[8] Dom David Knowles called him "the Erasmus, the Johnson of the twelfth century."[9] Even a study that challenged his vaunted knowledge of the classics concluded that "he may still be regarded as one of the most learned men of his time."[10]

These glowing assessments are based chiefly on John's two major works: *Metalogicon* and *Policraticus*, both dated from 1159. The former, in four books, is a detailed "defense of logic," which includes celebrated passages on the schools and masters of Paris in John's time. It assails "Cornificius" and his coterie of anti-intellectuals, and includes an affirmation of John's close friendship with Pope Adrian IV, his countryman. *Metalogicon* is also an important source for the famous aphorism about "dwarfs seated on the shoulders of giants" attributed to Bernard of Chartres.[11]

The *Policraticus sive de nugis curialium et vestigiis philosophorum* (On the Trifles of Courtiers and the Footsteps of Philosophers), in eight books has been described as "the philosophical memoir of one of the most learned courtier-bureaucrats of twelfth-century Europe."[12] The text ranges widely over a host of themes in disparate fields of philosophy and political science. The earliest books exhibit a satirical purpose and treat of courtiers and their

8. W.T.H. Jackson, *Medieval Literature: A History and Guide* (New York, 1966) 68; Staunton, *The Lives of Thomas Becket*, 7.

9. David Knowles, *The Evolution of Medieval Thought* (Baltimore, 1962) 135.

10. Janet Martin, *John of Salisbury and the Classics* (Ph.D. diss., Harvard University, 1968) 198. For a summary, see *Harvard Studies in Classical Philology* 73 (1969) 319–321.

11. *Metalogicon* 3.4. For an amusing history of the aphorism, see Robert K. Merton, *On the Shoulders of Giants: A Shandean Postscript* (New York, 1965). Serious treatments include Edouard Jeauneau, "Nani gigantum humeris insidentes: Essai d'interprétation de Bernard de Chartres," *Vivarium* 5 (1967) 79–99, and Brian Stock, "Antiqui and Moderni as 'Giants' and 'Dwarfs': A Reflection of Popular Culture?" *Modern Philology* 76 (1979) 370–374.

12. Nederman, *John of Salisbury*, 51.

trifling pursuits such as hunting and gambling, as well as such disreputable types as soothsayers and flatterers; the middle books focus on good government and contain John's well-known analogy of the officers of the state and the members of the human body; the final books survey philosophical doctrines in a general search for virtue and wisdom. The entire *Policraticus*, replete with classical and scriptural references and graced by wit and humor, bears witness to John's vast learning and serious purpose.

John of Salisbury's earliest literary effort, in verse, is partially a product of his student years. The *Entheticus de dogmate philosophorum*, a satirical/didactic poem of 926 elegiac distichs, begins with school themes and proceeds to mockery of courtiers. This shift supports the view that the *Entheticus* was a work in progress to which John added over time until about 1155, and some have considered it merely a verse preface to his prose works.[13] Recent scholarship, however, has shown this longer poem (there is, in fact, a shorter *Entheticus in Policraticum*) to be a distinctive, challenging work in its own right.[14] The satirical passages (ll. 1300–1752) on the perils of court life, the dangers lurking in hostels and among innkeepers, and even sketches of certain vicious rascals – all concealed under pseudonyms – at Canterbury, the poem's "home," are especially amusing.

John of Salisbury also left a substantial collection of letters. Many of these are "official" correspondence written in his capacity of secretary to Archbishop Theobald, but there are also numerous (later) personal epistles to friends and acquaintances that reveal John's sense of humor, integrity and Christian humanism. John also occupied some of his time in exile (1164–1170) with the composition of a historical treatise, *Historia pontificalis*. Its modern editor/translator referred to this incomplete book as "a fragment

13. Hans Liebeschütz, *Medieval Humanism in the Life and Writings of John of Salisbury* (London, 1950) 19–22.

14. Ronald E. Pepin, "John of Salisbury's *Entheticus* and the Classical Tradition of Satire," *Florilegium* 3 (1981) 215–227; Rodney Thomson, "What Is the Entheticus?" in *The World of John of Salisbury*, 287–301; Cary J. Nederman and Arlene Feldwick, "To the Court and Back Again: The Origins and Dating of the *Entheticus de Dogmate Philosophorum* of John of Salisbury," *Journal of Medieval and Renaissance Studies* 21 (1991) 129–145.

of papal history," but also commented on its historical value and described it as "a source of the first importance" on England during the civil wars between the Empress Matilda and King Stephen, the Second Crusade, and the character and policy of Pope Eugene III.[15]

As our brief survey of John's extant writings illustrates, he contributed to several literary genres in both verse and prose, but he does not seem to have been naturally drawn to biography or hagiography. Perhaps this is the reason, coupled with the haste with which they were composed, that led to the "disappointing" results of his efforts in depicting the lives of Anselm and Becket. Nevertheless, both are contributions by a major Anglo-Latin writer to what in his day was a burgeoning genre. Certainly they deserve scholarly consideration.

Moreover, into both *Lives* John wove favorite themes that he had fully articulated in earlier writings. In these instances we observe him applying his theoretical views and principles to actual circumstances. For example, John was an ardent champion of Church liberty. He feared the aggrandizement of royal power. In *Policraticus* (especially chs. 4-6) and in his correspondence, he often revealed his theoretical and practical resistance to the infringement of royal authority on the prerogatives and privileges of the Church. The conflicts included appointments to vacant episcopal sees, legal jurisdictions, revenues and the roles of clergy and laity in the governance of the commonwealth. As background to these complex issues was the Investiture Controversy, a dispute that began in 1075 with a papal decree forbidding lay investiture of prelates, i.e., the act of conferring insignia of office. This precipi-

---

15. Marjorie Chibnall, ed. and trans., *The Historia pontificalis of John of Salisbury* (Oxford, 1986) xxx and xl–xlvi. See also Roger Ray, "Rhetorical Scepticism and Verisimilar Narrative in John of Salisbury's *Historia Pontificalis*" in *Classical Rhetoric and Medieval Historiography*, ed. Ernst Breisach (Kalamazoo, MI, 1985) 61–102. The ascriptions of two other works to John of Salisbury, a prose treatise called *De septem septenis*, and a short poem, *De membris conspirantibus*, have been discredited, though the latter piece on the conspiracy of the limbs against the belly addresses a theme that he found attractive. Ronald E. Pepin, "'On the Conspiracy of the Members,' Attributed to John of Salisbury," *Allegorica* 12 (1991) 29–41.

tated an open conflict between Pope Gregory VII and the Holy
Roman Emperor, Henry IV, which resulted in the submission and
humiliation of the latter. The struggle, however, spread throughout Western Europe and lasted until 1122, when a compromise
was reached by the Concordat of Worms. One undisputed result of
the crisis is that papal power was expanded in both spiritual and
secular realms. In England, disputes in these matters between
Anselm, King William II, and later Henry I, twice led to the archbishop's exile; quarrels with Henry II caused Becket to flee into
exile for six years.

John of Salisbury was also an unflinching foe of tyranny in all
forms, a theme that was already evident in his earliest work, the
Entheticus de dogmate philosophorum (ll. 1299ff.). His extreme
expression of the doctrine of tyrannicide occurred in the *Policraticus* (Bk. 3.15), where he defined a tyrant as a "public enemy."[16]
Now, in the *Lives of Anselm and Becket*, John could illustrate
tyrannical behavior in practice. He reminds readers repeatedly
that both archbishops were persecuted for the sake of Church
liberty, and both bravely confronted tyrannical rulers. He described Thomas Becket as a "man of invincible constancy," one
who "fought even unto death to defend the law of his God and to
cancel the abuses of ancient tyrants."

John of Salisbury linked the themes of ecclesiastical freedom
and oppressive tyranny even more explicitly and extensively to the
conflict between Saint Anselm and King William Rufus, "a man
vigorous at arms, but insufficiently just or pious." His view of that
king is entirely negative, and as John traces the deteriorating rela-

16. John's teachings on tyrannicide have sparked a debate and a vast
literature of their own. Comprehensive discussion and complete bibliography
may be found, for example, in Cary J. Nederman, "A Duty to Kill: John of
Salisbury's Theory of Tyrannicide," *The Review of Politics* 50 (1988) 365–
389; Cary J. Nederman and Catherine Campbell, "Priests, Kings, and
Tyrants: Spiritual and Temporal Power in John of Salisbury's *Policraticus*,"
Speculum 66 (1991) 572–590; Richard H. and Mary A. Rouse, "John of
Salisbury and the Doctrine of Tyrannicide," *Speculum* 42 (1967) 693–707;
Jan van Laarhoven, "Thou Shall *Not* Slay a Tyrant! The So-called Theory of
John of Salisbury" in *The World of John of Salisbury*, ed. Wilks, 319–341;
Kate Langdon Forhan, "Salisburian Stakes: The Uses of 'Tyranny' in John of
Salisbury's *Policraticus*," *History of Political Thought* 11 (1990) 397–407.

tions between monarch and archbishop, he employs increasingly hostile epithets to characterize the former, who is described as "brutal," a "tyrant," and several times as "impious." John reports his death by declaring that "He who had lived like a beast met a bestial end."

In fact, John's final pronouncement on the violent death [murder?] of the king in the New Forest affirms his theory of tyrannicide: "Certainly whoever did this faithfully obeyed the will of God, Who had pity on the misfortunes of His Church."

Life of Anselm

Although John of Salisbury's *Life of Anselm* is far from a literary masterpiece, the work is important as an example of twelfth-century hagiography. It illustrates contemporary perceptions of holiness, standards of sanctity and methods of presentation employed to support an appeal for canonization at a time when more and more public cults of saints, approved by local bishops, were being submitted to the pope for universal recognition. The common elements of veneration by the faithful and translation of the saint's remains were being supplemented by *vitae* bearing witness to the virtues, heroic sufferings and miracles of the saint. John's *Life of Anselm* is one such work; it warrants close scrutiny and rewards it with valuable insights into the organization and development of a case for sainthood.

First, we must acknowledge that John's work is extensively dependent on the *Vita Anselmi* of Eadmer, a monk of Christ Church, Canterbury, and close friend of Anselm, published more than a half century before John wrote his *Life*.[17] From Eadmer he derived all his information about the numerous visions and miracles associated with the saint, save one that occurred after Eadmer's work was completed. He also gained knowledge of the

---

17. R.W. Southern, ed. and trans., *The Life of St. Anselm* (Oxford, 1972). Alain Nadeau, "Notes on the Significance of John of Salisbury's *Vita Anselmi*," in *Twenty-Five Years (1969–1994) of Anselm Studies*, ed. Frederick Van Fleteren and Joseph C. Schnaubelt (Lewiston, NY, 1996) 67–77. The author calls John's *Vita Anselmi* "an *abrégé* of Eadmer's intimate account of the life of Anselm."

archbishop's personal sufferings of mind and body, and of his public conflicts and humiliations in the service of God and His Church and even borrowed a few illustrative anecdotes from Eadmer. With this ample supply of information at hand, John then composed his own affirmation of Anselm's sanctity, which he underscored with a careful blending of several components: miracles, visions, virtues, sufferings, epithets and links to saints and Scripture.

The miracles attributed to Saint Anselm in life and *post mortem* are described for the most part in less detail by John than by Eadmer. They include cures effected by Anselm's cincture and by crumbs from his table, as well as those brought about by his prayers and blessings alone. Twice Anselm miraculously halted devastating fires. Through his intercession storms were calmed, a spring was discovered, and a packhorse that had fallen into the River Thames was saved with all its baggage intact. When the saint was being anointed for burial, balsam flowed abundantly from a nearly empty jar, and his inadequate coffin was miraculously enlarged to receive his body. John of Salisbury reports only one miracle that does not appear in Eadmer's writing: the total cure of a man named Elphege who, from birth, had been "blind, deaf, mute and lame." All of these miracles are included in John's narrative to affirm the sanctity of his subject.

Visions, likewise, confirm Anselm's holiness. These include Anselm's own prophetic visions concerning himself and others, such as the childhood dream in which he received dazzling white bread from the hands of the Lord, or the revelation concerning the final judgment on a monk he had fostered. Recorded also are dreams of others involving Saint Anselm such as that of an innkeeper who was warned repeatedly not to lie on a bed in which so great a guest as Anselm had slept. The most notable visions for John's purpose in the *Life* are those of monks and others who claimed that at the time of his death they observed the archbishop welcomed into Paradise. Outstanding among these is the story of a novice who prayed at Anselm's tomb and had a vision of an open book in which was written the words "Saint Anselm." The devout young man realized thus that Anselm's name had been entered in the Book of Life, and that he was most worthy to be called a saint.[18]

A saint's virtues and heroic sufferings are always included in hagiographical writings. Foremost among Anselm's manifold virtues were humility and charity. John of Salisbury's *Life* underscores these with numerous examples, and also specifically credits the saint with the monastic virtue of contempt for the world. In several places John offers examples of Anselm's kind and gentle manner. He even recounts two instances of his charity toward animals. In these charming anecdotes taken from Eadmer, the saint rescued a hare fleeing from hounds when it took shelter beneath his horse, and on another occasion he wished fervently that a little bird bound by a cord might be released. Immediately the cord broke and the bird flew away.

Of course, Saint Anselm's virtues fortified him and sustained him in his sufferings. With complete resignation to God's will he bore physical infirmities and serious illnesses during his life, and he had to endure many trials in his offices of prior, abbot and archbishop. The faithful discharge of his duties earned for him at times the hostility of two English kings and their henchmen, including many bishops. King William II and Archbishop Anselm had several serious disagreements, only two of which are mentioned by John: the recognition of Pope Urban II and the payment of aid demanded by the king. These disputes led to Anselm's voluntary exile from 1097–1100. After King William II's death, Henry I invited Anselm to return to England, but a confrontation over the issues of homage and investiture led to another exile in 1103. A compromise reached in 1107 called for ecclesiastics to render homage to the king, while he in turn agreed not to invest them with the insignia of office.

Following Eadmer (ch. 14), John of Salisbury reports that even members of Anselm's own household were disloyal to him and took advantage of his gentle nature to benefit themselves. Neither

---

18. This story is taken from the account of Anselm's miracles appended to Eadmer's *Life* (Southern, 168), where the modern translator has rendered *decentissime scriptum* as "written in handsome letters," rather than "written most deservedly" or "most worthily," which I think is the correct sense.

author, however, names individuals. Anselm was twice exiled and found no peace, John writes, except when he immersed himself in the cloister. John even reports that Anselm used to employ a particular analogy to describe his situation: "So is an owl happy in the nesting-hole with its chicks, but when it comes out, the ravens and crows lacerate it and tear it to pieces."

In recording all of the foregoing – miracles, visions, virtues, sufferings – John follows Eadmer, though his treatment is selective and far less detailed. But John departed from his predecessor's style and substance in other ways as well. Writing fifty years after Eadmer and with the specific intention of securing a papal canonization, John makes wide and varied use of epithets to define Anselm's holiness. Eadmer's work, begun in Anselm's lifetime and extensively revised later, usually refers to him simply by his given name, although near the end of the *Life* and in the brief description of miracles appended to it, Eadmer repeatedly uses the expression "Father Anselm." By contrast, from the very outset of his biography, John of Salisbury calls Anselm "blessed" and "holy," terms that were interchangeable. He specifically identifies Anselm with those whom God has sent to dispel the darkness and to illuminate His Church. These holy ones John calls "sons of the apostles and prophets." Once established, this link is reinforced and reiterated throughout John's *Life* by epithets. "Blessed Anselm" is hailed as an "apostolic man"; a "servant of God"; "the Lord's anointed." Moreover, in several instances John adds the word "true," confirming him as the "true worshipper of God"; "true follower of the Apostles"; "true disciple of Christ." Often he is referred to simply as "the man of God" or "the saint of God."

Besides the use of epithets, John also employs his substantial rhetorical skills to portray Anselm as a saint through allusions to other saints and the liberal use of quotations from Holy Scripture. He likens him to the Apostle whom Jesus loved [John 20.2] or to Samuel, who mourned for Saul [1 Samuel 15.35]. In his ministry Anselm became like Saint Paul, "all things to all men," [1 Corinthians 9.22] and at his death "he fell asleep in the Lord" [Acts 7.59] like Saint Stephen. When his prayerful petition for favorable winds was answered, he was recognized as the "vicar of Him Who commands the winds and the sea" [Matthew 8.26], and the miraculous enlargement of his stone sarcophagus is viewed as the gift of the Savior at whose passing rocks were split [Matthew 27.51]. These scriptural references are pervasive and serve as another means by which John of Salisbury affirms the holiness of Anselm, who, as John declares, "did not hold the ways of men as his example for life, but the word of God."

Finally, John places Anselm securely in the company of saints by invoking the names and deeds of seven of them in his narrative. Right from the Prologue, where John proclaims that it is a great source of perfection to have known who Anselm was (as was said of Saint Antony), he reminds his reader of apostles, prophets and saints to whom Anselm bears resemblance. John emphasizes his similarity to Saint Martin in three separate chapters, surely because Martin was the patron of Tours, where the petition for Anselm's canonization was presented to the pope. John also compares Anselm's gift of prophecy to Saint Benedict's, his charity to Saint Nicholas'; signs of divine favor and consolation in Anselm's life parallel events in the lives of Saint Clement and Saint Basil. John even borrows from Eadmer the story of a Canterbury monk named Elias who, in a vision at the time of Anselm's death, saw the archbishop conversing with a holy predecessor and fellow-monk, Saint Dunstan.

In May 1163, Archbishop Thomas Becket presented his petition for Anselm's canonization, supported by John of Salisbury's *Life of Saint Anselm*, to Pope Alexander III. Overwhelmed by petitions and the pressures of business, the pope delayed his decision and referred the matter to a provincial council for consideration. As a result, Anselm's formal canonization was postponed for over 500 years. By then, John's *Life of Saint Anselm* had receded into relative obscurity, for only a single manuscript, copied nearly 350 years after the *Life* was written, survives today.[19] Thus, the work was certainly not widely circulated; it is not mentioned by John's contemporaries, nor did he speak of it in his own letters. Surely the concise nature and restricted purpose of the text (i.e., to serve

19. This manuscript, Lambeth MS 159, was written in 1507 by Richard Stone, a monk of Christ Church, Canterbury.

as a canonization brief) contributed to its limited reception. Those who sought a fuller examination of Anselm's life and work would naturally have turned to the more expansive, intimate account by Eadmer, a work read in public as part of the lectionary of Christ Church Cathedral.

Life of Thomas Becket

John of Salisbury's *Vita S. Thomae Martyris* is the earliest of nine extant biographies of Saint Thomas Becket composed within seven years of his brutal murder in Canterbury Cathedral on 29 December 1170. In fact, the *Life* is based on a lengthy letter (no. 305: *Ex insperato*)[20] that John wrote in the early months of 1171 detailing the horrific event and its surrounding circumstances, and was probably written soon after. It was eventually supplemented and used as an introduction to Becket's collected correspondence, which was assembled by Alan of Tewkesbury in 1176.

Although labeled a disappointment, the work is important because it contains the earliest eyewitness account of the assassination, an assessment of Becket's life and activities as chancellor and archbishop by a knowledgeable, observant friend, and definitive declarations of his sanctity. If John of Salisbury did not bring his famous erudition to bear on this hasty composition, he did at least ably sketch the portrait of a contemporary saint.

John's Prologue opens with several images that signal the dominant themes of his *Life of Becket*: Holy Church; blood; freedom. Throughout the text that follows John underscores these points by revealing Becket as a guardian of the Church who is willing to shed his blood in defense of ecclesiastical liberty. The archbishop, he declares, was a sharer of tribulation and suffering for Christ, and so he must be a co-heir of consolation and glory in Him. Moreover, Becket is doubly deserving of an eternal crown because he also performed the office of teacher and model for his flock.

Becket's early years are disposed of quickly in John's *Life*. The author describes his physical attributes and highlights certain

---

20. W. J. Millor, SJ, and C.N.L. Brooke, eds. and trans., *The Letters of John of Salisbury* (Oxford, 1979) 2: 724–739.

pleasing qualities in the youth – tall stature, acute intellect, handsome appearance, amiable ways – but also acknowledges that he "courted the popular breeze." John immediately likens his subject to Saint Brice,[21] who was proud and vain and acted foolishly at times, but who must be admired and imitated for his bodily chastity. Becket's years of service to Archbishop Theobald are also surveyed rapidly. His tenure as chancellor to King Henry II is more detailed. The passages that treat of his life at court, where he was overwhelmed by afflictions, threatened by malicious men setting snares to trap him, where he had to struggle without ceasing against the "beasts of the court," resemble the satirical verses of John's *Entheticus*. Although Becket had to battle not only the young king's perverse advisors but even Henry himself to ensure the king's safety and honor, and to secure the well-being of the Church, his grace and diligence preserved him, and he found favor with the king through his magnanimity and loyalty. Thus, confident that his chancellor was well-suited for the exalted rank of archbishop of Canterbury, and that he would submit to the royal will, Henry made the fateful decision to nominate the reluctant Becket to the vacant see when Theobald died.

John emphatically makes the point that Becket's election to the archbishopric brought about an immediate change in his manner of life.[22] He borrows from Pauline epistles to assure readers that Thomas "put off the old man" and that he "put on the hair shirt and the monk, crucifying his flesh along with its vices and concupiscences." John's declaration that Becket "put on" the monk is significant, since long-standing tradition held that the archbishop should come from the monastic ranks. In fact, his esteemed

21. A former monk, Brice, or Britius, turned to a lavish lifestyle. He later reformed his ways and succeeded Saint Martin as bishop of Tours in 397. He died in 444.

22. The very notion of a moral "conversion" by Becket, the view promoted by John of Salisbury and, later, William of Canterbury, has been greeted by modern skepticism, and even cynicism. David Knowles reviews this tradition in *Thomas Becket* (Stanford, 1971) 53–55.

predecessors – Lanfranc, Anselm, Theobald – had all come from the Benedictine monastery of Bec in Normandy.[23]

John devotes ten chapters of varying lengths to Becket's tenure as archbishop of Canterbury. After a lengthy discourse on his charity, holiness and integrity, our author addresses the growing conflict with Henry II, which he describes as a dispute "between the King and the Church." He portrays Becket as a "man of God" and a "man of invincible constancy" amidst all the tribulation and travail of the councils at Northampton and Clarendon, the flight from England and the years of exile on the continent.[24] Throughout these passages John emphasizes by repetition that the archbishop acted consistently as a "confessor of Christ," "Christ's bishop," and a "future martyr." Upon his return to England after reconciliation with the king, he was received by the clergy and people as an "angel of the Lord."

The recent assertion that John's *Vita S. Thomae Martyris* is "very slight ... in fact little more than an expanded version of a letter written shortly after the murder" is not quite fair.[25] To be sure, John borrowed almost *verbatim* from his letter *Ex insperato* to recount the events of 29 December 1170. One should find no fault with this, since the letter is the earliest account of the historic murder, and a vivid description as well. It dramatically records the

---

23. Barlow asserted (*Thomas Becket*, 75) that "John of Salisbury's rhetorical claim that Thomas on becoming archbishop also put on the monk and hair shirt ... must be rejected."

24. Soon after his accession to the archbishopric on 3 June 1162, Thomas Becket's relations with king Henry II began to deteriorate. Their dispute over jurisdiction in legal and ecclesiastical matters was exacerbated when Becket refused to affix his seal to the Constitutions of Clarendon, the documents adopted at a council of the realm at Clarendon in January 1164 affirming "royal customs." At Northampton in October of that year, the archbishop was summoned to answer various charges, including embezzlement during his tenure as royal chancellor, an accusation clearly calculated to humiliate him. This tumultuous trial concluded with cries of "traitor" hurled at Becket by barons of the realm; it was the final break between him and the king that led to his exile. He fled from Northampton, clandestinely made his way to the coast and sailed across the English Channel on 2 November 1164. Becket remained in exile on the continent for the next six years.

25. Michael Staunton, *Thomas Becket and His Biographers* (Woodbridge, 2006) 20.

dialogue between the archbishop and his assassins, his final words, his demeanor in death and the outrage perpetrated on his body by one of the knights. The letter reports the aftermath of the murder, when the assassins, "with insatiable avarice and astonishing boldness," plundered all they could find of the martyr's belongings. The passages borrowed from John's letter that are incorporated into the *Life* conclude with a brief account of the hasty burial and the cures already being effected at Becket's marble tomb.

The suggestion that John of Salisbury's *Life of Becket* shared a similar purpose with his *Life of Anselm*, that is, to support a claim of sanctity and to secure canonization by the pope, is certainly plausible.[26] If so, it apparently met with success. Archbishop Thomas Becket was canonized by Pope Alexander III on 21 February 1173, Ash Wednesday, little more than two years after his murder in the cathedral.

Translation

In rendering John of Salisbury's *Lives of Anselm and Becket* into English, I have sought to adhere as closely as possible to the original Latin without producing a wooden or cumbersome translation. I have taken liberties with the text only to facilitate reading, such as eliminating some transitional adverbs which impede the flow of English, or breaking up certain lengthy sentences into shorter ones. I trust that the result is an accurate expression of the mind of John, a Christian humanist whom I have long admired. I also hope that this translation, which now makes his entire corpus of writings available in English, will prove useful to students without Latin who wish to read the lives of two notable saints of Canterbury composed by a leading scholar of the twelfth century.

For the *Life of Saint Anselm*, I used the edition by Inos Biffi, *Vita di sant'Anselmo d'Aosta* (Milan, 1988). His text is based on an edition published by Henry Wharton in 1691 and reprinted in J.A. Giles, *Joannis Saresberiensis Opera Omnia* (Oxford, 1848) 5: 305–357. This is also the text printed in J.P. Migne's *Patrologia*

26. Ibid., 25.

Latina 199: 1009–1040. My translation of the *Life of Thomas Becket* is based on the text printed in J.C. Robertson, *Materials for the History of Thomas Becket*, Rolls Series 67 (1875–1885) 2: 301–322.

The Life of Saint Anselm

God works wondrously to dispel the shadows of faithlessness and error, and so from the beginning of the formation of the world He has dispensed His mercy always and everywhere to procure for His Church capable servants through whom it might advance toward virtue and, having passed through the waves of this transient world, might sail to glory. For just as in the darkness of night, while some stars are setting, others are rising to brighten the world, so for the purpose of constantly illuminating the Church, sons succeed their fathers. Through them the knowledge and worship of God are perpetually preserved from generation to generation. These holy men are indeed the sons of the apostles and the prophets; just as they succeed them in faith, so too they receive the inheritance of virtue and wondrous works, and they attain the glory of eternal reward. Among these Blessed Anselm, the archbishop of Canterbury, shone forth like the brightest constellation. And not only did he illuminate the Latin world, but he spread the rays of his light into the Greek world at the Council of Bari (over which Urban, the Roman pontiff, presided), refuting the detestable error of the Greeks concerning the procession of the Holy Spirit.

If anyone wishes to consider how great a man he was (which I do not doubt to be advantageous to anyone), let him diligently read the books which he wrote for various reasons, and his letters; let him read over the history written about him and the recent kings of the English;[1] also, the two books which Eadmer, a venerable monk and priest, very truthfully published in a clear style about his life and manner of living, as one might expect of a religious man who had been a very close associate of his.[2] Let him read also about the miracles which the Lord worked wondrously after his passing, and let him revere the visitations of the Most High which happen frequently in memory of him. In any case, I am not afraid to proclaim publicly what another before me said about Antony:[3] that it is a great source of perfection to have known who Anselm was. Thus, resorting to the aforementioned books, through the mercy of the Lord (Who does not always keep sinners from being heralds of His glory), I have taken care to narrate some things about the life and manner of living of so great a father, with sufficient succinctness and plain enough speech so that if someone cannot aspire to the fullness of all which has been written by him or about him, at least from this drop of so great a stream he can taste how good, how sweet is the Lord;[4] how blessed and how indispensible was Father Anselm who worshipped Him faithfully.

Chapter One

ON THE FATHER AND MOTHER AND CHILDHOOD OF ANSELM, AND ON HIS VISION.

Anselm was born in the city of Aosta.[5] His father was Gundulph, his mother Ermenberga, one of the women of discretion. From the beginning of his life he conceived a fear of the Lord, from which

1. John here refers to Eadmer's *History of Recent Events in England*.
2. Eadmer, a monk of Christ Church, Canterbury, was a friend and companion to Anselm from 1093 until the latter's death in 1109.
3. Saint Antony of Egypt is regarded as a founder of monasticism and the outstanding example of the "desert fathers." He died in 356. His biography by Saint Athanasius is John's source here.
4. Psalm 33.9.
5. When Anselm was born in 1033, the city of Aosta in northern Italy was part of the kingdom of Burgundy.

consequently he brought forth the fruit of his own salvation; from this afterward proceeded works of true justice. Thus, Anselm strove all the more to imitate the ways of his mother, for since the care of the whole household fell to her (his father was occupied with other matters), she managed everything wisely and devoted herself to works of mercy. She often visited the church with diligent zeal, praying and receiving God's words with complete eagerness of mind, and faithfully following the precepts of wisdom. Indeed, she communicated what she had heard to others in a pleasing report, and she encouraged herself and others to devotion.

From her the boy heard – and believed – that God was the sole creator of all, reigning in Heaven, the bestower and rewarder of good things, and already at a tender age he aspired to the knowledge of God. Like a child, however, he thought that Heaven was attached to the nearby mountains and that the palace of God, about Whom he had heard, was there, and that He dwelt there bodily with the angels and saints. One night in his dreams it seemed to him that he ascended to that place and that on the slope of the mountain which he was climbing he saw the servants of God gathering wheat, but very carelessly, so that, inflamed by his zeal for the faith, he was determined to accuse them before God over this. He climbed up and found God sitting alone in His palace, except for a lone steward through whom, after he was summoned and was sitting at the feet of the Lord, he received (as He commanded) the most dazzling white bread. Immediately he ate of it and was filled. He related the vision to his companions and boasted that he had been fed with divine bread, believing for a time that these things had been done corporally.

From then on he was intoxicated with so great a love of God that, despising the whole world, he even longed for some serious infirmity, on the pretext of which he could be received in a community of monks, which he very much wanted. And indeed, according to his wish, he became ill, just as he prayed for, but his father, as it was then thought, opposed his becoming a monk. However, the truth is that the Lord was saving him for something else. At any rate, he applied his mind to learning and to upright living, and, advancing in both beyond all his contemporaries, he accomplished many things in a short time.[6] When he became a young man, after his mother had died, he decided to go to Gaul, drawn by his eagerness for learning (he was inflamed by an immense desire for this), and so that with the help of flight he might at least avoid the displeasure of his father, who treated him harshly. But while he was leaving his homeland, and almost fainting in the ascent of a mountain due to toil and hunger alike, he ate snow so that his strength might be restored to him in this way. The servant whom he had as the sole companion of his journey, pitying him, began to search diligently for some food in the pack which a little ass was carrying, and immediately, contrary to expectation, he found a very fresh loaf of bread. He did not know who had put it there. And so Anselm was refreshed for his journey and his toil, giving thanks to God for His gift.

Chapter Two

CONCERNING THE DEEDS OF ANSELM IN BURGUNDY, FRANCE AND NORMANDY. ANSELM FOLLOWED THE COUNSEL OF THE ARCHBISHOP OF ROUEN AND BECAME A MONK AT BEC.

The three years thereafter were spent partly in Burgundy, partly in France; in Normandy Anselm approached that Lanfranc whose memory is held in joy and pride, a man noted for learning and virtues, a man whose way of life was excellent in all things, and one to whom all who were seeking advancement in eloquence or wisdom were flocking from diverse parts of the world to hear, for he was held to be preeminent in the judgment of all.[7]

And so Anselm became closer to him in friendship than others, and, so to speak, he drank in the spirit of his master. He was

6. Wisdom 4.13.
7. Lanfranc was born in Pavia c. 1010, but moved to Normandy as a young man. He became a renowned teacher and monk at Bec, where he served as prior for almost twenty years before he was chosen to be abbot at St. Etienne in Caen. He preceded Anselm as archbishop of Canterbury from 1070–1089.

totally occupied with letters, and these he learned or he taught without interruption. He devoted himself to this purpose, persisting in hunger and thirst, in cold and nakedness,[8] indeed persisting with such great steadfastness in study, that it seemed the kingdom of Heaven could be bought for less. Thus, coming back to his senses and wisely examining his ways, he discerned that one thing was necessary,[9] and that a stream of eloquence or this world's philosophy does not confer true happiness. These often produce pride (*tumor*); they never or rarely produce fear (*timor*) of the Lord, which is the beginning of wisdom.[10] Sometimes learning represses certain vices and brings contempt for the world, but clearly contempt for the world is useless where the love of God does not grow strong. He was inspired all the more after he learned of his father's death, and although he directed his spirit altogether toward the service of God, yet he remained in doubt as to which way he might choose. Indeed, he was uncertain whether to seek out a hermitage or a cloister of monks or, constructing a house from his own inheritance, to minister to strangers and the poor according to his means, for his mind was fluctuating among these three. So that fickleness might not sway his decision (from which follows repentance, the servant and constant attendant of deeds not done rightly), he revealed the agitation of his mind to Lanfranc, and on his advice he went to Maurilius, the venerable archbishop of Rouen, to seek his opinion on this matter, for he was thought to possess the Spirit of the Lord.[11] And so, based on the counsel of him who preferred the monastic life to all others, Anselm became a monk at Bec in the twenty-seventh year of his life.

The prior of this place was the abovementioned Lanfranc, under the holy abbot Herluin, who built the church at Bec from its foundations out of his own inheritance.[12] From these men Anselm received the rudiments of the monastic profession. Forgetting those things which were in the past and ever-exerting himself

8. 2 Corinthians 11.27.
9. Luke 10.42
10. Psalm 110.10
11. Maurilius, formerly a monk at Fécamp, served as archbishop of Rouen from 1055–1067.
12. Herluin founded the monastery at Bec in 1034.

toward the things that lay before him according to the model of the Apostle,[13] he strove to fulfill the role of monk, and he devoted himself to emulation of the holy monks with such great diligence that in a short time he would resemble the more perfect ones. Indeed, in three years he made such progress that he could justly seem to all to be the clearest example of true sanctity and monastic perfection.

Chapter Three

LANFRANC, PRIOR OF BEC, IS PROMOTED TO ABBOT OF THE MONASTERY OF CAEN. ANSELM SUCCEEDS HIM AS PRIOR OF THE MONASTERY OF BEC. ON WALTER TIREL, AND ABOUT THE GREAT STURGEON WHILE HE WAS DINING WITH ANSELM.

After Lanfranc was promoted to abbot of the monastery of Caen, Anselm succeeded him as prior of the church at Bec [in 1063]. By virtue of having obtained honor and rank, he strove to make progress also in religion and more faithfully to serve God, to Whom he vowed his obedience. Now crucified to the world and its desires,[14] he contemplated the things of Heaven, and in his work he only occupied himself with those things that avail to eternal life, for he did not hold the ways of men as his example for living, but the word of God. In fact, as he himself used to say, Divine Scripture is the best model for living well. There are four sources from which the streams of justice could flow to him, namely: constant meditation on God's law; careful carrying out of God's law; faithful reporting of God's law; devout prayer. For what is more perfect than to meditate on the law of the Lord day and night;[15] to carry out the mandates by which the prophet rejoices that he has understanding;[16] to make known the glory of God,[17] Whom fishermen

13. Cf. Philippians 3.13.
14. Galatians 5.24
15. Psalm 1.2
16. Psalm 118.99–100.
17. Psalm 95.3.

proclaimed and became renowned in the teaching of the truth and confounded the philosophers of the gentiles? Occupied in these activities, Anselm consecrated his obedience to the Lord with devout prayers, punishing himself by great fasting to repress in this way the attraction of food, namely, that from the beginning of his tenure as prior he would experience no delight in food or drink at all. But he did not suffer hunger from fasting, for he had already lost the pleasure of eating.

The prayers which he wrote[18] indicate how great his devotion was, and if anyone examines his book of meditations, he would discover this clearly. What was written of Martin[19] is most certainly true of Anselm: that Christ was never absent from his mouth, whether [his subject was] justice or peace or whatever pertains to the true life. He kept ever before his eyes the fear of the Lord, and he dreaded every appearance of sin more than anything which could be named, to such an extent, indeed (as he used to acknowledge), that if he physically perceived the pain of Hell on this side and the wickedness of sinning on that side, and if he needed to pick one of the two, he would prefer to be thrust into Hell than to be involved in sins. And he used to declare another thing: that he preferred to be held by Gehenna [and be] an innocent man than to hold the kingdom of Heaven as one made filthy by sin.

He offered this reason for his assertion: God loves the innocent and good wherever they might be, and, on the other hand, He hates and detests all wickedness. Assuredly, the Highest Justice does not make the wicked blessed, and the Highest Goodness by no means makes its friends wretched. Anselm was benevolent so that he might disburse his paternal affection to all. He searched the ways of true knowledge so that he might read reliable writings and emend [textual] corruptions in books, which, as a general

18. For Anselm's prayers and meditations, his earliest writings, see *The Prayers and Meditations of St. Anselm*, translated by Benedicta Ward (Harmondsworth, 1973).

19. As a young soldier, Saint Martin of Tours gave half of his military cloak to a freezing beggar at Amiens, and the next night he saw, in a dream, Christ wearing the half-cloak. This famous story is found in the *Life of Martin* (2.27) of his friend and biographer, Sulpicius Severus, John's source here. Saint Martin died in 397.

rule, were very many at that time. He attributed this authority to
Divine Scriptures: that whatever they asserted, he acknowledged
to be most true. Indeed, nothing deflected his strength of spirit
away from the profession of truth and the cultivation of justice. A
Spirit of Counsel[20] was thriving in him, so that those who were
forlorn streamed toward him in droves from all sides. The face of
Truth shone upon him with such great clarity and copiousness that
he wisely understood the mysteries of Scripture, he effectually
untied the knots of disputed questions, he frequently made known
the secrets of hearts, and by a certain gift of prophecy he very often
predicted events hidden in the future. It happened that on a certain night before the nocturnal vigils, while Anselm was medita-
ting, he wondered how the prophets saw things past as well as
future, but also those that were absent as if they were present, and
how they faithfully and confidently made them known. And while
he was totally absorbed in these questions, he saw through the
walls of the chapel and dormitory how the sacristans in the church
were preparing the altars and candles, and how one of them was
ringing the bell to waken the others. While they were rising, he
marveled, concluding that it was very easy for God, Who had confounded nature and led the rays of his eyes through the thickness
of walls, to reveal hidden things to His prophets and saints.

When necessity compelled him to stop at the lodging of a poor
monk who was complaining vehemently about the lack of fish to set
before so great a guest (for he had nothing in the house except
bread and cheese), Anselm said: "Brother, do not be troubled over
the want of provisions – God will provide these for us – but,
quickly, put your net into the nearby river, and you will catch a fish
which will suffice for us all." The monk reluctantly obeyed Anselm's
order, because it seemed incredible and a clear tempting of the
divine majesty, but at last, to the immense astonishment of all, a
fish of wondrous size was caught, just as the man of God had said.

Another time when the nobleman, Walter Tirel,[21] was detaining
him so that he might dine with him, he was distressed and com-

20. Isaiah 11.2.
21. Walter Tirel, lord of Poix in Picardy and Domesday lord of Langham,
Essex, will appear again in Chapter 12.

plaining about the scarcity of fish. Consoling the man over the want of delicacies, Anselm, the true worshiper of God, said: "Are you complaining, and a large sturgeon is now being brought to you?" The man laughed and was altogether disbelieving. At that very moment, just as Anselm had said, he saw a huge sturgeon being brought to him by two men who said that it had been found by his shepherds on the bank of the River Authie and sent to their master. Thus, just as is often said of Blessed Benedict,[22] so Anselm too is believed to have had the Spirit of prophesying.

Chapter Four

ANSELM RECEIVED DIVINE GRACE SO THAT HE COULD
PROMISE TO SERVE GOD WITH A PURE HEART AND
A GOOD CONSCIENCE. CONCERNING A CERTAIN MAN
OF DECREPIT OLD AGE. ON A CERTAIN YOUTH
WHO WOULD NEVER TOUCH HIS PRIVATE PARTS
FOR ANY REASON. CONCERNING OSBERN THE MONK.
CONCERNING A CERTAIN BROTHER WHO WAS
HATEFUL TOWARD ANSELM. ON THE VISION
OF RICULF THE MONK.

The Spirit of Wisdom directed Anselm so that nothing delighted him except God, to Whom he referred all things; he perceived the beginning, progress and end of virtues and vices, and expounded on each and how they could be secured or avoided. He fulfilled the role of an apostle to such an extent that if the circumspection of humility had not restrained him, he could have professed openly with the Apostle from a pure heart and good conscience and true faith:[23] "Who is weak, and I am not weak? Who is scandalized, and I am not on fire?"[24] And what we know to have been written about [John,] the disciple whom Jesus loved, that whatever he said was

22. Saint Benedict, abbot, is the patriarch of western monasticism and author of the *Rule of Saint Benedict*. He died at Monte Cassino c. 547.
    23. 1 Timothy 1.5.
    24. 2 Corinthians 11.29.

warmed by the fire of love,[25] so also Anselm, although he does not rise up to equal so great an apostle, nevertheless followed his footsteps with diligent zeal so that his whole speech, whole life and all his writings seemed to be inflamed by the fire of divine love which shines in them. You would think that he lived not for himself, but for others; indeed, the more usefully he lived for others and the more faithfully he lived for God, the more truly he lived for himself. While seeing to the advancement of others, he acquired divine grace for himself. In fact, although he attended to the salvation of all, yet he paid greater attention to those who were weakened by age or illness, and to young people. Indeed, his charity hastened more quickly to and more freely aided the needy person, and he had more compassion for the one who was suffering more severely. Thus, in accordance with his wish, it happened to him very frequently that the sick gained strength, the aged were comforted, sinners were recalled to the fruit of a better life, young people advanced and became firm in the cultivation of true virtue. For, "A jug will long keep the smell with which it was once imbued when new,"[26] and the habits with which tender youth is imbued are dislodged with more difficulty and not without a certain sorrow.

Let us expound on these successes of his by a few examples. Herowald, a very old man laid low by such weakness that he had control over his tongue alone and could not take food nor drink, was awaiting imminent death, as it was thought, in the infirmary. He regained his strength from wine which Anselm gave him to drink from his own hand and which he had squeezed from a cluster of grapes into the palm of his hand.

A certain youth bound himself to a resolution of ill-advised zeal, so that on no occasion would he ever put his hand to his genitals. But since it often happens that a more serious temptation follows ill-advised vows, such great pain assailed him in those parts that a leaden mass seemed to be hanging there. Unable to conceal this, he was advised by Anselm to examine the kind of infirmity it was with his hand; out of respect for his vow, the brother refused. And so the servant of God, knowing that to the pure all

25. Gregory I, *Homilies on the Book of Ezekiel*, 2.3.21.
26. Horace, *Epistles*, 1.2.69.

things are pure,[27] summoned a very aged brother and with him led the youth to a solitary place. His flesh was found to be completely well, and from the time his flesh was inspected by the holy man, all pain departed and did not trouble the youth further.

A certain Osbern, a monk by profession, a youth in age, was sharp in intellect and skillful at handicrafts, but he had such evil habits that one could rightly give up hope of his salvation. He used his dog's tooth, so to speak, and assailed Anselm with insatiable hatred. But Anselm had pity on his mistaken ways. He won over his boyish spirit with a certain saintly shrewdness, at one time soothing his bitterness with gentleness and at another tolerating his childish deeds as much as the rule of the order allowed. Often using prayer or exhortation, rarely commands, Anselm did not so much snatch away the evil of his ways as steal it away, and somehow he bound the unknowing youth with the coils of divine law. He first curbed his hatred of everything, later extinguished it, and then summoned forth his affection toward himself; little by little he sowed seeds of charity in the now-cultivated heart, and he nourished there genuine shoots of love. Thus by kindness and benevolence he procured the young man's prompt obedience, so that the youth who did not accept counsel (*verba*) from anyone before, now embraced even whippings (*verbera*). The one who had been most perverse of all now surpassed all those of his same age in proceeding from virtue to virtue, and in a short time he resembled the more perfect. Indeed, others could easily look to him as if into some mirror of divine grace which they might imitate and from which they might order their own way of life.

But then when the greatest fruit was expected for the Church, the young man was prevented by an untimely death, to the mighty sorrow and tears of all. When the youth had been carried into church according to custom, Anselm withdrew to a more private place of prayer while the others were occupied with prayers around the deceased. When he closed his eyes a little in sleep, as happens after sadness and tears, he saw persons distinguished by bright countenances and shining garments seated as if to pronounce judgment on his own Osbern, who was present

27. Titus 1.15.

and resembled a man whom either too much blood-letting or
weakness had made pale. When Anselm inquired solicitously
what sentence he had received, Osbern responded: "Three times
the ancient serpent rose up against me and three times he fell
back, and finally the bear-keeper of the Lord set me free."
Probably he had been accused three times as one who could be
charged, through the Ancient Enemy's false report, of original sin
before baptism, of actual sins committed later before he became
a monk, and of violation of his monastic profession. I think that
the good angel, who restrains and punishes hostile powers, is
called the bear-keeper, who extricated this monk from the false
accuser's noose by reason of his faith, the charity he retained,
and his penitence at the end. Moreover, while Anselm was sitting
by Osbern's sickbed and ministering to the needs of his soul and
body, and with his great love of serving assumed the duties of
others, it had been agreed upon between them that, if it pleased
God, Osbern might reveal to him his circumstances after death.
The dead Osbern showed to the living Anselm the manner of
obedience which he had undertaken with zeal while alive.
Perceiving from this vision that Osbern had a hope of salvation
and could be helped by the intercessions of the saints, Anselm
took care that the host of the divine sacrament was offered on
Osbern's behalf every day of the entire year by himself or by
another. Also, after he had sent letters all around, he saw to it
that the monks [in other monasteries] offered private prayers
and solemn services for Osbern. Thus it happened that all were
seeking a good outcome for Osbern, and Anselm's kindness won
over more people for the Lord than if he had ruled with strictness
and power.

Nevertheless, he sacrificed nothing of the vigor of the monastic
life, but he was more inclined to mercy than to severity. For if he
had to be condemned for one or the other, as he used to say, he
would prefer to be found too merciful in the sight of God rather
than too cruel. Indeed, he knew that authority and austerity produce fear rather than love. Neither is there order without love,
since there is no true religious life without charity. Surely you will
not obtain love by force; mutual trust bestows this, a simple grace

bestows this. While always devoting himself to works of charity and mercy, Anselm procured much fruit for the Lord.

Since he was much vexed in the meantime by the tumult of affairs, he decided to give up the office of prior. But when Maurilius, archbishop of Rouen, was consulted, he ordered him a second time, by virtue of obedience, to bear the yoke imposed on him to the end, adding by this same authority that he not resist Divine Providence when he was called to greater works. For the archbishop asserted that he had very often seen many who, when they fled pastoral care for the sake of their own peace and quiet, always went from bad to worse while walking in idleness. With sadness and sighing, Anselm obeyed, and entrusting himself wholly to God, he strove to serve the interests of his brothers entirely.

Although he wished to accommodate all and injure no one, and was peaceable even with those who hated him,[28] yet he could not avoid the envy which either his virtue or happiness, or his reputation for those things, always inflamed. For those who had entered the order before him used to mutter that a novice was preferred to them. One of these, whom no amount of deference could appease, was brought to the point of death. While he was in that state, he began to grow pale and to tremble and, hiding his face in a strange manner, to turn it in different directions. When his brothers asked the reason, he said that two huge wolves were killing him with their bites. This was reported to the prior. After going apart for a little while into his accustomed chapel, he returned to the infirmary, and with his hand stretched forth he made the sign of the holy cross, saying, "In the name of the Father and of the Son and of the Holy Spirit." After this was done, the sick man grew still and said that when Anselm entered and stretched out his hand, he saw a fiery lance shoot forth from his mouth toward the wolves. It drove the terrified wolves away in swift flight. The servant of that Spirit, Which was bestowed on the Apostles in fiery tongues,[29] approached the sick man. He led the brother to penance and confession, and absolved him, predicting with a certain power of prophecy even the hour in which he would pass away.

28. Psalm 119.7.
29. Acts 2.3–4.

One night when a certain Riculf, who performed the duties of sacristan, was passing by the door to the chapterhouse as he was about to go into the dormitory, he looked in and saw a brother at prayer surrounded by a ball of fire. He went away astonished by this strange phenomenon, but did not find Anselm when he looked for him in his bed. He went back and found the servant of God at prayer, but that ball of fire had now disappeared. A ball of fire had distinguished Martin as he celebrated Mass,[30] so too did one surround Anselm as he prayed. The Apostles received the Holy Spirit in fiery tongues, so too did this same Spirit dart forth in fire on the tongue of Anselm. He also commanded demons, drove out diseases, foretold the future, performed and taught the law of God, and in many ways he was shown to be an apostolic man.

Chapter Five

IN THE MONASTERY AT BEC, ANSELM WROTE SIX BOOKS: *ON TRUTH; ON FREE WILL; ON THE FALL OF THE DEVIL; ON THE GRAMMARIAN; MONOLOGION; PROSLOGION.* ANSELM IS STRICKEN BY SERIOUS ILLNESS, DURING WHICH HE IS TAKEN UP IN SPIRIT. ON A CERTAIN ABBOT WHO CAME TO ANSELM SEEKING COUNSEL. ON BOYS RAISED IN THE CLOISTER. ON A CERTAIN KNIGHT NAMED CADULUS.

During this time Anselm wrote three books: one *On Truth*, another *On Free Will*, the third *On the Fall of the Devil*. He also wrote a dialogue whose title is *On the Grammarian*, and another he called *Monologion* (because in it he alone speaks), in which what faith proclaims about God is proven by reason, and all the authority of Divine Scripture is passed over in silence.[31] He also

---

30. In *The Miracles of Saint Martin* (1.12), Gregory of Tours describes Saint Martin surrounded by a ball of fire as he officiated at the altar.

31. Anselm completed the *Monologion* in 1077 and sent it to Lanfranc for his approval. In this work he developed proofs for the existence of God based on degrees of perfection.

wrote a sixth book, whose title is *Proslogion*,[32] in which he briefly demonstrates that those things which are said about God according to Himself, like almighty, good, and all other attributes of this kind, are one in Him. But when he was so distressed in his search for this proof that his anxiety not only banished sleep but also food and drink, so that out of a certain desperation he ascribed this search to temptation, suddenly during his nighttime vigils what he was seeking became clear to him. He wrote his thoughts down on tablets and entrusted them to a keeper. But it always remained uncertain who stole them, since they could be found nowhere. He rewrote his opinions on other tablets, but when they were sought again later from their depository, they were found on the pavement in front of the place where they were stored with their wax torn off and scattered in pieces. It is still unknown who did this, unless it was the malice of the Ancient Enemy, which is believable. Therefore, it was set down a third time on paper, and so it has remained.

Then Anselm was stricken by a serious illness during which, transported in spirit, he saw a great river rushing headlong. Into it were flowing filthy things of all kinds, squalor and every kind of uncleanness. It also carried off all the furnishings of the world which it could touch, men and women, old and young, poor and rich together. But when Anselm was feeling pity for those whom, he heard from his guide, must be fed and given drink from such filth, "Do not be amazed," he said, "for this stream is the world, which sweeps away worldly men." And the guide also added: "Do you wish to see what a true monk is?" And when Anselm said yes, he led him into a cloister whose walls were overlaid with the purest silver, and there was a meadow of silver covered with fresh grass of wondrous fragrance. And although the bent grass gently yielded to them when they rested there, the crushed grass arose again when they stood up. When Anselm was seized with the desire to dwell there, the guide said: "Now, do you wish to see what true patience is?" When Anselm requested that with great

---

32. The *Proslogion* also aims to prove the existence of God, and in it Anselm affirms (ch. 1) that his faith seeks understanding in the famous exclamation: *Credo, ut intelligam*: "I believe in order to understand."

eagerness, the guide disappeared, and Anselm woke up. Indeed, it is likely that he was restored to his former condition so that in the tribulations which he was to suffer for the Lord he might show what true patience is. For from that time on he always abhorred the world and its delights more and more, and he more zealously and ardently embraced the true monastic life.

As a result, men seeking fellowship or assistance or counsel streamed toward him from all over, even from remote regions, as if to some fountain of religion. Among these came a certain pious abbot. When he had spoken about many matters, at last he sought counsel concerning the boys of the monastery. "We are accomplishing nothing," he said, "by chastising them all day, for they are perverse and incorrigible, and they are becoming ever worse." "And how are those who are now adults?" Anselm asked. "Sluggish and bestial," the abbot replied. "You have performed laudably," Anselm said, "for you have shaped a man, the image of God, into a beast! Don't you know that a plant which is confined from the outset by unyielding obstacles on all sides in no way rises to a lofty height? It does not put forth deep roots nor raise up branches unless it has some freedom. Heat needs to be tempered by moisture so that the sprouts of seeds might grow strong. Otherwise the heat destroys them, the moisture dissolves them. In order to fashion a splendid image out of silver, the hammer needs not only an anvil, but a graving tool, a pad for beating metal, and other things with which the artisan's task is accomplished. One does not care [for sheep] by shearing alone. Who takes away milk and starts out little ones on more solid foods? Indeed, this would be to choke them, not to feed them. Where does one progress who begins at perfection? Wax that is hard does not accept the image of a seal, and wax that is too soft and liquid does not retain it. Talk about the subtlety of spiritual things with him who has grown very hard through worldliness and he will not accept your words on account of his hardness. A small boy does not even understand what you are saying. An intermediate age, situated between these extremes, can do both. Thus, youth is easily molded if it has an experienced craftsman, and it faithfully retains the likeness of its education. For that reason, too, one labors more usefully in these young people, according to the Apostle,[33] if they are prepared for solid food with milk first, and if they take single steps at an appropriate pace. But you demand of them that they rejoice in tribulations, that they love their persecutors, and similar things which are ascribed to the distinctions of the perfect. And so, just as love casts out fear,[34] so inordinate fear casts out love. Thus it happens that the suspicious, the complainers, the grumblers, the envious, the ambitious and the faithless nurture wicked, prickly thoughts, and those who experience no love in their superiors bear no love toward them or others. And as much as they grow in extension of the limbs in the body, by just so great an increase are vices extended in the mind. Would you want this to happen to you? Your justice, I would put it no other way, is on view to all." Anselm was accustomed to teach by tested ways and common examples, and to speak so that his words might benefit the hearers, not so that he might seem to know many things and seem eloquent. He also took great pains in teaching them when he held any teaching position because their instruction could either benefit or injure all who were subject to him. When he heard these things, the abbot sighed and openly confessed that he had strayed from the way of truth.

Meanwhile, Abbot Herluin was weakened by a serious sickness, and the management [of his monastery] was entrusted to Anselm. Horses and other necessities for travelers were prepared specifically for his use. But when he heard the word 'ownership,' he became very frightened and ordered everything to be shared with his companions. He did not want anything to be called his own, but wished that everything might be a common possession for himself and his brothers. Thus he rejected all that was so offered to him, even that which the devotion procured of those who undertook this so that they might know the man.

On a certain day when Anselm went into the dormitory to his bed, he found a little gold ring. To this day it is not known whose it was or where it came from, but it is believed to have been a sign of his future bishopric. The devil envied the salvation of many which

33. Hebrews 5.13–14.
34. 1 John 4.18.

the servant of God brought about. He even laid ambushes for those who flocked to him from every quarter. To pass over others in silence for the present, a certain knight named Cadulus became devout and offered himself entirely to the Lord in prayer. And behold, he heard a voice outside the church like that of his squire wretchedly lamenting that the horses and all his possessions had been snatched away by robbers. Yet the knight persisted in prayer, regarding the loss of his devotion of greater value than the loss of his property. The Enemy, aggrieved over the steadfastness of the devout knight, assumed the shape of a bear and, rushing down from the ceiling in front of him, he tried to hinder Cadulus as he prayed by the terror of his fall and his frightful appearance. But the persevering knight remained unconcerned and laughed at the monster. Finally, he came out of the church. As he was walking he heard a voice saying clearly to him: "Cadulus, where are you going? Where are you going, Cadulus? Why do you go to the prior, that hypocrite? He will strip you of your goods as is his custom and will hurl you into a fount of error. Surely you will be sorry then, since his reputation is far removed from his way of life." But hearing the voice and seeing no one, having fortified himself with the sign of the cross and prayers, he came to Anselm and, on his advice, Cadulus put on the monk's habit in the monastery at Marmoutier in the district of Tours. Anselm was accustomed to send to that place each one whom he chose under the Lord's inspiration, for very often regret followed those who went to other places.

Chapter Six

HERLUIN, ABBOT OF BEC, DIES. ANSELM SUCCEEDS
HIM AS ABBOT OF THE MONASTERY AT BEC.
THE UNCERTAINTY OF ARCHBISHOP LANFRANC
CONCERNING WHETHER SAINT ELPHEGE WAS A MARTYR
OR NOT. THE QUESTION IS POSED TO ANSELM, ABBOT
OF BEC. ANSELM'S RESPONSE TO LANFRANC'S QUESTION
ABOUT THIS MATTER.

Anselm succeeded Abbot Herluin when he died.[35] He was reluctant and resisting, but was constrained by the brothers and especially by the urgent order by which Maurilius, archbishop of Rouen, had bound him. However, so that he might have time for prayer, reading and the office of the Word, he delegated legal cases and external matters to brothers suited to this. He commanded that they always choose to suffer rather than to commit fraud, and that to the best of their abilities they avoid disputes altogether without enormous loss, for lawsuits are seldom if ever prosecuted without a loss of charity. When Anselm was forced to attend legal cases, he rarely spoke, except about morals or the Word of Life; moreover, disdaining the subtleties of malicious accusations, he often slept. But once awakened, he so exposed the deceits which they contrived as if he had heard them from those confessing them or had found them written sometime in public records. He showed such great kindness to guests that he often plundered the refectory for their sake. He harbored such great hope in God's mercy that he never seemed to think about tomorrow. It also came to pass for him in accordance with his faith that his monastery always abounded in all necessities. And just like a second Nicholas, the gem of priests,[36] he overflowed with a heart of mercy toward the poor to such an extent that in some way he seemed to know this alone: "Give to everyone who asks you."[37]

When Anselm came to England [in 1079] to inspect the monastery's possessions there and especially to see Archbishop Lanfranc, they had many conversations about various matters. Finally Lanfranc spoke about Blessed Elphege.[38] "The English," he said, "among whom we live, have established certain saints for them-

---

35. Herluin died on 26 August 1078 and Anselm was elected to succeed him a few days later. His formal consecration took place on 22 February 1079.

36. Saint Nicholas, a fourth-century bishop, was widely venerated during the Middle Ages. Dante alluded to his celebrated generosity in *The Divine Comedy* (*Purgatorio*, 20: 31-33), and his life was included in the *Golden Legend* of Jacobus de Voragine. Nicholas is the patron saint of children, and his story gave rise to the legend of Santa Claus.

37. Matthew 5.42.

38. Saint Elphege, also called Alphege, was archbishop of Canterbury; he was martyred on 19 April 1012.

selves whose merits are doubtful. One of these reposes in our church, namely Elphege, who is our predecessor. He was indeed a good man, whom they honor not only as a saint but also as a martyr. However, when I investigate his cause, I find that he was stoned by the pagans and finally killed with an axe after many injuries, insults and whippings for this reason: he refused to extort money which was demanded of his people to ransom him. And so, since the punishment does not make a martyr, but the cause does,[39] I earnestly wish to hear your opinion on whether the English should be restrained or followed." As a newcomer in England, Lanfranc did not yet know the story completely, for Elphege also suffered for Christ. Yet Anselm responded to what he had heard. "He seems to be an illustrious martyr," he said, "who preferred to die rather than to inflict harm, especially on those whom he was obliged to protect. And clearly one who dreaded so much that which seems a small matter would have remained most faithful in acknowledging Christ, for he who avoids the least offenses does not readily give in to weighty ones. So, therefore, just as John [the Baptist] is considered a glorious martyr who suffered for truth, so also Elphege seems to me to be a glorious martyr who suffered for justice, since each suffered for Christ, Who, just as He is truth, so also is He justice." Lanfranc acquiesced. He ordered the martyr's story to be read and his feast to be solemnly celebrated each year.

Anselm traveled about not only to churches and venerable sites, but to cities and castles and homes of noblemen, invited and drawn here and there. A true follower of the Apostles, he brought the word of faith and salvation to all. He became all things to all men so that he might win over all to such a degree that even to those who were without the law he himself was without the law, so to speak.[40] Yet, although he concerned himself unceasingly with the law of Christ with all zeal, no one was terrified of him on this account; all venerated him and many followed him. Every age, every profession, every class listened to him teaching to their advantage, and they accepted Anselm. Even the king who had sub-

39. Augustine, Sermon 275.1.
40. 1 Corinthians 9.19–22.

jugated the English, although he was a source of fear to all, yet he was subject to him.[41] The Lord confirmed his words by the following signs: he cured the sick and, with nature yielding to the Creator, he is known to have cured a leper. A nobleman on the border of Flanders and Ponthieu was suffering with this infirmity. He was instructed in a vision to drink the water with which Anselm, abbot of Bec, had washed his hands in the celebration of Mass. This was done and he was restored to health on the spot. Another man from the community at Bec was cured of a powerful illness when he was sprinkled with water purified by Anselm, for he had been instructed to do this in a dream when he was suffering almost at the point of death. At about this time a man praiseworthy for his erudition in literature and his integrity of morals, Boso by name, was joined to the community of monks by Anselm, but in a short time he was so tempted that he was distracted by his thoughts and had no rest at all. Finally, after several days he revealed to Anselm what he was enduring. But with the loving compassion of a fellow-sufferer, Anselm replied: "May God watch over you," and from that time all the temptations of his mind departed. It would take long to report how many sick people he cured, but especially those with fevers, either by the imposition of his hand or by water or bread blessed by his hands. It is well-known and true that many sick people regained their health as a result of the leavings from his table.

Chapter Seven

ON THE GLORIOUS KING, WILLIAM THE FIRST. HE DEPARTS FROM THIS LIFE. HIS SON WILLIAM RUFUS SUCCEEDS HIM IN THE KINGDOM OF ENGLAND, A MAN INSUFFICIENTLY JUST OR PIOUS. ANSELM WRITES THE BOOK *ON THE INCARNATION OF THE WORD*.

41. John refers here to William the Conqueror.

When the glorious King William died, his son William, whose surname was Rufus, succeeded him.[42] A man vigorous at arms, but insufficiently just or pious, he was wasteful of his own property, grasping at others', very fond of wild beasts but very unconcerned about people, a promoter of warfare and wickedness but a most vehement oppressor of the Church and innocence, an enthusiastic devotee of pleasure, as one might expect of one in whom love of the world and contempt for God flourished equally without moderation or measure. But what is most unbecoming a prince, he had no respect for his body and debauched himself by every kind of uncleanness. Not only the nobles, but even the common folk, although they were ill used, followed the prince as much as they could, as usually happens, since it is well known that such as the ruler of a country is, so are those who dwell in it. Indeed, the world adapts to the example of the king. Edicts are not able to alter human feelings so much as the life of the ruler does.[43]

As a result when the Church was suffering on all sides, its hardship was all the more severe because there was no one to place himself as a wall before the house of the Lord.[44] When the venerable father Lanfranc was translated from this world to the Lord, in the fourth year of this persecution, Anselm, invited by the nobles and compelled by the Church, went to England.[45] Arriving at Canterbury on the day before the nativity of the Blessed Virgin Mary, he departed very early in the morning because people on all sides, as if predicting the future, declared that he would be archbishop. From there he proceeded to the court and was received honorably and amicably by the king, who came to meet him. After a few words were spoken between them, Anselm advised that everyone be sent out. And so setting aside his own concerns, he thought to attend to public business. Speaking one to one, he

42. King William II was crowned on 26 September 1087. He was called Rufus ("reddish") because of his ruddy complexion. His relations with Anselm were often stormy.

43. Claudian, *Panegyric on the Fourth Consulate of Honorius Augustus*, 298.

44. Ezechial 13.5.

45. Lanfranc died in May 1089; Anselm arrived at Canterbury on 7 September 1092.

revealed what was being said privately and publicly, and he stood up to the king face to face, for he did not bear the oil of the sinner which hirelings rub soothingly on the heads of rulers who go astray.[46] They parted from each other and after a few days the king became gravely ill. Affected by weakness and moved by the counsel of wise men, he gave his assent for Anselm to be promoted to archbishop, calling him most worthy of the highest honor and an illustrious preacher of the truth.

And so, though unwilling, Anselm was swept along [into being appointed archbishop] in the year of grace 1093 on the 6th of March, the first Sunday of Lent. On the following Easter Sunday, when he was at Winchester, the town began to be consumed by a sudden conflagration. Since the fire seemed sure to surround the guesthouse, the mistress of the house was warned by friends to remove her possessions. She responded that she was not afraid, but was safe due to the presence of so great a guest. She was in no way willing to agree to remove anything. Moved by her, therefore, two venerable men, Gundulph, the bishop of Rochester,[47] and Baldwin the monk, Anselm's administrator,[48] made him at least view the conflagration and oppose it with the sign of the saving cross. A wondrous thing! He extended his hand and the flames fell. The fire, which had invaded the house, left it, half-burned, as if it did not dare to proceed while Anselm forbade it.

Though he resisted election for a long time, he was finally compelled to consent, and on the 4th of December he was consecrated at Canterbury by all the bishops of England. This saying of the Gospel was found concerning him: "He invited many and sent his servant at the supper-hour to tell those invited to come, for now everything was prepared. And they all at once began to excuse themselves."[49]

46. Psalm 140.5.
47. Gundulph was an old friend of Anselm's from Bec. He served as bishop of Rochester from 1077–1108.
48. Baldwin, a monk of Bec, was an adviser and friend to Anselm. He served as head of the archbishop's household until Anselm's death in 1109.
49. Luke 14.17–18. These *"sortes Christianae"* were taken at the election of bishops. The verses portended difficulties and strife for Anselm. Cf. Barlow, *Thomas Becket*, 73, concerning the bad omen at Becket's election.

Then Anselm proceeded to court and joyfully spent three days of the Lord's nativity. From that time on the king harbored a very great indignation toward him because Anselm was unwilling to pay a thousand pounds of silver,[50] since he wanted to be promoted to the archbishopric without any bribery and compliance and intervention. Departing from there, he went to his manor called Harrow, and there he consecrated a parish church. A certain clerk from London who was associated with the bishop's attendants fled after secretly taking a vessel for chrism during the proceedings. But by the Providence of God he went back and forth so often, wandering in utter ignorance of the road he had known so well before, that he confessed his guilt, exposed by this clear indication of his wandering. He returned the vessel and afterward took the road which leads to London without any straying.

A few days later, Anselm returned to court, summoned there to fortify the king by his blessing for he was about to cross the sea. During that time, while the wind was contrary, Anselm strove to win over the king for the peace of his churches, mildly admonishing him not to allow the law of God to be trampled by royal authority.[51] As a result the king became irritated and ordered him to leave, and prohibited Anselm to wait there any longer for him to cross.

From that day on the Church of God was even more harassed; its possessions were reduced and taken away, its people were intimidated by lawsuits and costs, and day by day the situation went from bad to worse. Everyone who was inflicting injury wished that his evil deeds might be well known, for, like Sodom, they rejoiced in the disclosure of their sin.[52] Indeed, whoever offended Anselm seemed to render a service most pleasing to the king. He had no

50. Fearing any suspicion of simony, Anselm refused to make a monetary offering to the king in return for his munificence in granting the archbishopric to him.

51. In a letter to Archbishop Hugh of Lyons soon after the king's departure, Anselm outlined the contentious issues: the king's demand for a contribution of funds to support his expedition to Normandy; his recognition of Pope Urban II; the calling of an ecclesiastical council; a question of knight's fees owed the archbishop.

52. Isaiah 3.9.

peace, except perhaps when he immersed himself in the cloister. Making a comparison of this kind, he used to say with tears: "Just as an owl is happy in the nesting-hole with its chicks, but when it comes out, the ravens and crows lacerate it and tear it to pieces, keep yourselves within as much as is permitted, most beloved sons. It is enough that worldly affairs and anxieties consume me as their owl." Even the members of his household were in large part opposed to him.

He was so indisposed toward worldly affairs that whenever, out of necessity, he took part in secular cases for any length of time, he either became disheartened or incurred some serious illness. He was incapable of taking part in the reckoning of accounts, but the care of all these matters fell to Baldwin, about whom we spoke. Thus as often as it was allowed, he went to a more secluded place and did not cease from divine conversations and prayer day and night, not even while eating. During this time he wrote the book *On the Incarnation of the Word*, which was written in the epistolary style, and which the Roman pontiff of the Church approved.[53] In fact, Urban even employed arguments taken from it against the Greeks at the Council of Bari.

Chapter Eight

HOW ANSELM WENT TO THE KING, HUMBLY PETITION-
ING TO GO TO ROME FOR THE *PALLIUM*[54] NEEDED
TO ADMINISTER HIS OFFICE. ON THE DISTURBANCE AND
DISPUTE BETWEEN THE KING AND THE ARCHBISHOP
AND BISHOPS OF ENGLAND.

When the king returned from the lands across the sea [29 December 1094], Anselm went to him, humbly asking that, in accordance with the requirement of his office and ecclesiastical custom, he be allowed to go to Pope Urban for the *pallium*, without which he

53. Anselm started this work at Bec, revised it in the winter of 1092–1093 in England, and completed it in 1094.
54. The *pallium* is a vestment conferred on archbishops by the pope.

could not fully administer his office. But at the name of Urban, the king became angry, declaring that no one in his realm ought to name a pope not of the king's choosing.[55] A day and place were set for the archbishop to respond concerning this rashness.[56] The parties were present, and all applauded the king's wishes. The bishops especially very shrewdly urged that no pope be accepted in the kingdom of England unless the king had chosen beforehand. When Anselm, wishing to render to Caesar the things that are Caesar's and preferring to obey God rather than men,[57] restrained them with canonical and clearly divine reasons, with a single impulse they cried out that he had offended the royal majesty and had put his own laws before the will of the king. Indeed, those miserable men did not dare to ascribe anything even to God unless the king were consulted. Therefore, at one word from the king, certain bishops refused all obedience to their archbishop and renounced their participation with him in fraternal community, others [refused obedience] to the commands he enjoined upon them on behalf of Urban, the Roman pontiff. All, except [the bishop of] Rochester alone, broke the bond of obedience and the faithful fulfillment of the promise they had made. Moreover, the king deprived the archbishop and his men of all security, and he declared his open hostility unless Anselm publicly professed that from then on he would not obey the Roman pontiff. But Anselm, persevering in the faith, sought from the king safe-conduct and permission to leave [England].

At length, through the intervention of noblemen, he obtained a truce of several months, and for the moment the king promised peace to him and his men. Yet, quickly abandoning the faithful

55. Urban II, a former prior at Cluny, was pope from 12 March 1088–29 July 1099. At a synod at Clermont in November 1095, he issued a call for the First Crusade. In 1881, he was beatified by Pope Leo XIII. King William did not recognize Urban as pope until 1095. He remained neutral in the dispute between the antipope, Clement III, and Urban, until the latter made concessions to him. These included the pope's accession to the demand that papal legates would require the king's permission to enter his realm.

56. The meeting took place at the royal castle of Rockingham in February 1095.

57. Matthew 22.21 and Acts 5.29.

fulfillment of what he had promised, the king expelled Baldwin from his realm and vehemently afflicted the archbishop with respect to his people and lands. Meanwhile Lord Walter, the bishop of Albano, brought the archbishop's *pallium*, and procured peace between the lord king and the pope.[58] He also brought it about that Anselm was admitted into favor by the king, at least for the sake of appearances.

A little while later, when the king had triumphed over the Welsh,[59] he sought a pretext and began to renew his dormant quarrels with the archbishop. Certainly in the matter of the succession [to fiefs in Canterbury lands] he was more insolent and almost unbearable. Anselm returned and once again sought permission to go to the lord pope. The king ordered him to desist from this undertaking since there was no reason, or an empty one, for this journey. Anselm's prudence needed no counsel, he said, nor did his purity need absolution.

When the archbishop was returning to his manor called Hayes, a hare which hounds were chasing sought protection under the hooves of the horse which the servant of God was riding. The father stopped, and the hounds in pursuit did not dare to come closer. All marveled and were astonished. The man of God felt pity for the unfortunate little beast, declaring that the soul of a sinner leaving the body was at stake. Then he raised his voice and ordered the hare to depart, and he restrained the hounds by the power of speech alone.

Another time he saw a little bird with its foot bound by a cord, and a boy holding the cord; sometimes the bird was drawn back, at other times given some slack. Anselm wished that the cord would break so that the little bird might be free. Instantly his wish was fulfilled, and the boy wept because the bird flew away. Anselm rejoiced and was glad for the bird; he added that the devil weeps in just such a way when those whom he held bound by the snare of

58. Walter, the cardinal-legate, presented the *pallium* to Anselm at Canterbury on 27 May 1095, some two weeks after the recognition of Urban II by King William.

59. King William's foray into Wales occurred between March and May 1097.

sin escape. Indeed, Anselm used to turn almost everything he had or heard or saw into a lesson for life.

Anselm was once again summoned by the king, and among other things he asked a third time for the permission he sought. The king was upset and complained that he was exceedingly annoyed. In his rage he ordered, through mediators, that the intemperate archbishop should leave the realm immediately without hope of returning or, giving up this undertaking, promise under oath that he would never appeal to Blessed Peter or the apostolic see in any matter at all. He added that if Anselm wished to remain, he follow the decision of the court not to persist in what he had asked of the king. To these statements Anselm replied: "He is lord. He says what he wants. But I go where necessity draws me. I must do that which I have professed, and obey the mandates of Him Whose ministry I carry on."

At these words the court was thrown into disorder. It declared Anselm guilty of lese majesty, reproached him and applauded its own resolution. But Anselm patiently bore the council's indignation, rejoicing that he was found worthy to suffer insults in the name of Jesus.[60] He went to the king with a calm expression and before his departure offered his blessing to him, if he should not refuse it. When the king bent forward and responded that he did not decline it, the archbishop blessed his persecutor from his heart and departed. Those who feared God saw Anselm off with their goodwill and wishes; as much as it was permitted, they supported him with prayers and commendations. The king, however, persisted in his ferocity, so that God seemed to have justly withdrawn from him.

Chapter Nine

ANSELM WAS SENT INTO EXILE. ARRIVING AT CANTERBURY, HE EXPLAINED THE REASON FOR HIS JOURNEY TO HIS OWN CONVENT OF THE CHURCH OF THE SAVIOR AT CANTERBURY [I.E. CHRIST CHURCH]. BEFORE THE

60. Acts 5.41.

HIGH ALTAR OF CHRIST HE TOOK UP HIS BAG AND STAFF.
WITH A BLESSING HE COMMENDED HIMSELF TO GOD
AND TO THE PRAYERS OF THE FAITHFUL. THE COMMEN-
DATION OF THE ROMAN PONTIFF TO ANSELM.

From there the archbishop went to Canterbury and received permission [to leave], first from his own brothers, then from the
shrines and all the clergy and people, after the reason for his
journey was made known publicly. And so, after he took up his bag
and staff before the altar of Christ according to the custom of pil-
grims, and he commended his sojourn to God and to the prayers of
the faithful; seen off by the almost inconsolable groans and tears
of all, he proceeded to Dover. There he found a certain clerk,
William of Warelwast, whom the godless king had sent to Anselm.[61] This man tarried for fifteen days at Anselm's table, and like
a member of the household he was involved in everything, going
in and out everywhere. He did not tell anyone why he was sent.
But when the sailors were urging Anselm to board ship and the
baggage was being carried on, behold, this same William, to the
amazement and indignation of all, detained the archbishop on
shore as if he were a fugitive and guilty of some crime. He opened
the bags and saddle-packs, and like a punctilious investigator, he
examined what they had in all their gear. However, the searcher's
carefulness was mocked: no money was found. Then, when Anselm was departing freely, the crowd watching saw him off with
prayers and tears, and hurled very harsh rebukes and curses at the
[king's] envoy as he left.

The travelers had barely gone a little distance on the sea and,
behold, the wind shifted. At first the sailors muttered, then they
openly complained and cried out to all that they must either go
back or die. When he heard this, Anselm wept profusely and
groaned. Having recourse to his accustomed support: prayer, he
said: "May God grant, may the Lord grant what He wills toward
me: may He thrust me back into my old hardships, or may He
allow me to proceed in His service, as I have determined to do

---

61. This man served as chaplain to King William II, and later to Henry I.
In 1107, he became bishop of Exeter.

under His inspiration, and cause me to do so, for I am not my own, but His." After he said these words, in an instant you would have recognized the vicar of Him Who commands the winds and the sea: a wind rose up behind them which swiftly drove the passengers with great joy to the desired shore. Furthermore, when the ship which had carried the archbishop was unloaded, a wondrous thing appeared, because in one plank a hole of almost two feet was found, but it did not let in any water at all while the holy man remained on the ship. But when the cruel king heard about the archbishop's crossing, he ordered all Anselm's possessions to be confiscated, and he rendered everything which Anselm had accomplished to be null and void.

Anselm, however, rejoiced in the exile imposed on him; he also recognized it as a pledge of future beatitude that the Lord deemed him worthy to suffer for justice. He felt pity for the hardships of the churches and the plight of his followers, whose calamities he would scarcely recount without tears as he faithfully bore that tempest in mind. But our faithful God, Who does not abandon those who put their trust in Him, attended the exile of His servant who was suffering for Him, so that whatever peoples or places he came to, he was received humanely, cared for kindly, treated properly, and listened to by all because of his reverent submission.[62] Indeed, a certain charm of divine sweetness shone on the very face of the man, so that he was loved by all, and the venerable gray hair of the old man who feared the Lord evoked respect and fear in equal measure in those who saw him. People of every age and sex flocked to him in droves in whatever places rumor announced his arrival beforehand so that they might deserve to obtain his holy blessing. Those who deserved to see nothing in his passing-by judged themselves fortunate [to see him]. His speech rooted in God was pleasing to listeners, and to those who feared the Lord it was sweeter than honey and the honeycomb.[63] The more he was honored, so much the more carefully did he guard the virtue of humility. A true disciple of Christ, when he was greatest

62. Hebrews 5.7.
63. Psalm 18.11.

of all, he lived among his companions as a subordinate, and the one who was superior acted just like a servant.

Proceeding as far as Lyons, Anselm waited there for the messengers whom he had sent to Rome, prevented from traveling by bodily sickness and certain other causes. When the messengers returned, he went to the Lateran, summoned by the Roman pontiff, and he was received with the greatest honor [in late April 1098]. The Church at Rome gave him thanks. Also, the Roman pontiff himself gave a long speech in the presence of the entire curia and the nobility who had gathered on account of so great an exile, and among other things, he said: "Although we ought to regard this man as a teacher most experienced in all the liberal disciplines and as one nourished and practiced in religion, and although he should rightfully be respected as some pontiff and patriarch from another part of the world, yet such sincere faith, such outstanding humility presides over his mind that he has been accustomed to consult us, who have more need of his counsel, and he could not be kept away by the dangers of land or sea from [showing] reverence for Saint Peter, whom he has visited." The Roman pontiff spoke these words and more, but in response to all Anselm remained silent out of prudence and fear of the Lord. But when the reason for his coming was made known, the Church marveled and was astonished, and it promised the fullest assistance. When Anselm was ordered to stay [in Rome], he fled from the inclemency of the Roman weather and went to the mountains. He was welcomed with honor by a venerable man named John, a former monk of Bec who was then abbot of San Salvatore Telesino, and was taken to his countryplace called Sciavi.[64]

Chapter Ten

ANSELM COMPLETED HIS BOOK *WHY GOD BECAME MAN* [*CUR DEUS HOMO*] IN THE PROVINCE OF CAPUA.

---

64. This town, about twenty miles northeast of modern Caserta in southern Italy, is now called Liberi.

ON THE SCARCITY OF WATER. ON THE WELL OF WATER.
ON THE DUKE OF APULIA. ON THE COUNT OF SICILY AND
THE FRIENDSHIP WITH POPE URBAN. ON THE COUNCIL
OF BARI. ON THE CONFUSION OF THE GREEKS AND
THEIR HERESIES. ANSELM IS CALLED A HOLY MAN
BY THE MEN OF ROME. ON THE INVESTITURE OF
CHURCHES. ON THE COUNCIL HELD AT ROME.

And so while Anselm was living there on the summit of the mountain where the country place was, refreshed by the healthy air and
by a certain solitude, he said: "This is the place of my rest; here
shall I dwell."[65] Devoting his time to God and to himself, he completed there in the province of Capua the distinguished book
that had been started in England which is entitled *Why God Became Man.*[66]

The inhabitants of the village were distressed by a scarcity of
water because springs, wells and cisterns were almost entirely
lacking to them. A single well on the slope of the mountain used to
provide relief for them, though slight, since each day before the
ninth hour it was so depleted that it supplied nothing from then
until the next day. But when the monk who was in charge there
ascertained by clear signs the holiness of the guest they had
welcomed, he made known their inconvenience. He begged assistance and said that water now had to be sought on the mountain
peak, which seemed to be the utmost foolishness. Anselm praised
his pious request. Thus Anselm was asked to choose the place, be
the first to break ground and then to beseech the Lord for running
water. Humoring him just like a second [Pope] Clement,[67] he fulfilled his host's request, and in a short time an abundant stream of

65. Psalm 131.14.
66. Anselm writes in the Preface to his book that he had started it in
England, and that parts were copied and circulated without his knowledge.
Finished in 1098, it offers rational arguments for the Incarnation of Christ.
67. Clement I was the third successor to Saint Peter. Banished to the
Crimea and forced to labor in the quarries, he miraculously produced a
spring of water for his fellow-workers. John's source for the legend is probably the anonymous fifth-century "Passion of Saint Clement," parts of which
found their way into the Roman breviary.

healthful ever-flowing water was found. Indeed, as the inhabitants say, the sick are cured of harmful infirmities when they have drunk the water that has been drawn. Even to this day that well, which is very copious and not of great depth, is called the archbishop of Canterbury's well.

At that time Roger, duke of Apulia, was besieging Capua,[68] and he made the man of God come to him. He received him with the highest honor and provided for him a suitable office in a certain chapel so that he would not hear the tumult from its remoteness to the army [but] from the nearness of it the duke visited him often each day. When Anselm was coming out of this place on a certain night while others were sleeping, he fell into an old cistern of great depth, and while falling he cried out loudly: "Holy Mary!" Running to him terrified almost out of their wits, his companions saw their father at the bottom. But he gave them a sign and indicated that he had suffered no injury, and he was lifted out altogether unharmed.

Urban, the Roman pontiff, came to him. In the guest quarters, they were so close to each other that almost everyone who came to Urban visited Anselm, for the reverence that majesty conferred on the former, sanctity conferred on the latter. Even the pagans who were serving the duke in his army were more deferential to Anselm, wishing him prosperity and saluting him, and very many of them would have converted to the faith through him had not fear of the duke and of the count of Sicily[69] held them back, for they were not permitted to come to the faith. After the siege was lifted, a council was held at Bari,[70] where Anselm refuted the Greeks by his catholic reasoning, and he taught that the Holy Spirit proceeds from the Father and the Son. From there he returned to Rome with the pope. Since the pope commanded it, Anselm received Englishmen who came to Rome at his feet, [kneeling] just as they did before the Roman pontiff. Anselm's humility rejected this until the pope ordered him, and thus he moderated his hu-

68. Roger, duke of Apulia from 1085–1111, was besieging Capua in order to restore Richard II, prince of Capua, to the city from which he had been expelled by its inhabitants.

69. Roger of Sicily was the uncle of Roger, duke of Apulia. He died in 1101.

70. The Council of Bari was held at the beginning of October 1098.

mility so that he might not impede the devotion of anyone who wished to do good.

Thereafter, seeing that more authority was conferred on Urban by his presence, the leading citizens of the city at times laid ambushes for Anselm out of loyalty to the emperor, who was persecuting the Church.[71] Yet, in order that it might be undisputed that he was the Lord's anointed and a true disciple of Christ, as soon as they saw him, they threw down their weapons and fell to the ground, and those who had approached to do evil sought the gift of his holy blessing. And so throughout the entire city the authority of his piety grew stronger, so that he was not called archbishop or primate, but "holy man" through *antonomasia*, that is, by virtue of his excellence, as if it were his proper name. Meanwhile, a council was held at Rome, and among its other decrees it was established that laymen who performed ecclesiastical investitures and those who accepted them at the hands of laymen would be punished by a sentence of excommunication. Those who presumed to consecrate in office someone who had received his honor in this way were also punished under the same sentence.[72]

Chapter Eleven

ARCHBISHOP ANSELM ARRIVES AT LYONS AND IS
RECEIVED WITH HONOR BY THE VENERABLE ARCH-
BISHOP HUGH. KING WILLIAM OF ENGLAND SENDS
MESSENGERS TO ROME. THE CASE BETWEEN THE ARCH-
BISHOP AND THE KING IS DEFERRED BY POPE URBAN.
ON THE DEATH OF POPE URBAN. ANSELM IS RECEIVED
BY GUY, THE ARCHBISHOP OF VIENNE. ON THE LAMENTS
OF TWO KNIGHTS. ON THE CRUMBS AT ANSELM'S TABLE.
ON THE FIRST, SECOND AND THIRD VISIONS
OF THE DEATH OF WILLIAM, KING OF THE ENGLISH.

71. Henry IV, the Holy Roman Emperor, supported the antipope, Clement III, and led military campaigns into Italy. He forced Urban II to surrender Rome in 1092.

72. The Vatican Council of 1099 prohibited lay investitures of prelates and forbad clergy to swear oaths of feudal allegiance.

From there Anselm returned to Lyons and was received by a venerable man, Hugh, bishop of the primary see of Gaul,[73] just as if he were lord of the place. As a matter of fact, the archbishop and bishops of the same province showed as much deference to Anselm in all things as if they were suffragans of the Church at Canterbury. Certainly in those days the Church at Canterbury found more faith among strangers than among its own people, for the sons persecuted the father, and the man's enemies were members of his own household.[74] Indeed, at their counsel, that William, whom we mentioned when Anselm departed from England, was dispatched by the impious king and came to Rome while Anselm was still living there. Among other things he obtained from Urban [an agreement] that he would defer the case of Anselm from Easter to the feast day of Saint Michael [29 September 1099]. For that reason the archbishop believed that the way of returning to England was closed to him as long as the king was alive. But the Guardian of Israel, Who does not sleep,[75] whatever human temerity might imagine, in the meantime dispensed a sentence of eternal judgment and removed Urban, who deferred the man of God's case at the request of a tyrant, from this world so that he did not see the appointed day.[76] Anselm, however, prospered in exile. Not only in Lyons, but also in the bordering provinces he was universally praised by all while God made him illustrious.

Invited for a visit by Guy, archbishop of the noble city of Vienne,[77] which is called the greatest city of Gaul, Anselm celebrated the feast of Saint Mauritius, which is a solemn one there on account of the presence of [the saint's] head. After the divine services, when they had sat down for refreshment of the body, two knights with tremulous voices and pale faces stood near him. Weak, their limbs almost withered, they begged that he might

73. Hugh was archbishop of Lyons, and a friend and frequent correspondent of Anselm's. He died on 7 October 1106.

74. Micah 7.6.

75. Psalm 120.4.

76. Pope Urban II died on 29 July 1099.

77. Guy was archbishop of Vienne from 1088–1119, when he was elected pope and took the name Calixtus II. He died in 1124.

deign to give them some crumbs of his bread. But Anselm said: "As I see it, you do not need crumbs so much as solid bread. The food is abundant and there is ample room. Go with my blessing and be seated. Eat as much as you want." He also added: "I shall do nothing else for you," knowing what they had intended, for he avoided doing anything that could be considered a miracle, since he sought not his own glory, but the glory of God, in all things wishing not for what was his own, but what was Jesus Christ's. Then one of those sitting at the right hand of the holy man, discerning their purpose, as if overcome by the insolence of those begging, seized morsels and offered them to the beggars, warning them to depart quickly so as not to vex the man any longer. They ate them and, departing with the man of God's blessing, they were immediately restored to health, cured of the quartan fever. This was made known by their own words.

One of the leading men of that region was troubled for a long time by this same malady. He was carried by his servants into the church of Saint Stephen, where Anselm was about to celebrate the divine rites. After he had heard Mass, he departed in good health. A few days later he thanked Father Anselm, declaring that he had been cured of the quartan fever by his blessing, and he received advice from him about his salvation. Instructed by these he lived, as is commonly known, more worthily before God, more acceptably to the world, and more usefully to himself.

At about this time a certain priest approached Anselm as he was on his way to Cluny. He asked that Anselm might deign to have regard for his sister, who had gone insane, and to bless her. But Anselm passed by as if he were deaf. The priest pleaded with him, and people came together from every direction and pleaded with him. However, he responded that God should not be tested in this way. But he was not allowed to go before he raised his right hand and made the sign of the cross that brings salvation over her. After this was done, he fled quickly and, putting his cowl over his head, he wept over the unfortunate woman's tribulations. She returned home and had not yet reached the threshold of her house when she was granted perfect health and caused all the people to speak in praise of the man of God.

Returning from there to Lyons, Anselm went through Mâcon, and there at the request of the bishop and clergy he celebrated a solemn mass in the church of Saint Vincent. In a public exhortation he counseled the people to beg the Lord in their prayers for rain, which the earth needed. They responded that they had done this often and had been often disappointed and begged him to help bring about what they needed and advance their wishes by his own prayer. The divine rites were celebrated, and through the office of their priest the prayers of the people were offered to the Lord. Without delay, the rains followed according to the wishes of all and sundry, and the whole city was effusive in their praise of the holy man. Arriving at Lyons, he wrote one book *On the Conception of the Virgin and Original Sin*, and another whose title is *A Meditation on Human Redemption*.[78]

While these things were being done, Pope Urban died before the first of August, and Anselm was left to the judgment of God alone. And although he suffered much and seemed very moved by the distress of his household, yet there thrived in him a cheerful disposition and episcopal authority because the guiding principle of the words and deeds of that One Who "in the beginning was the Word"[79] did not fail him or abandon him. Also, many things were predicted by many people concerning the death of the impious king. Because of evident signs and clear visions, these were seen as vindication for Anselm. He did not pay attention to them, but prayed to the Lord every day for the conversion and salvation of the tyrant. In the third year of his exile, during a conversation with Blessed Hugh of Cluny at Marcigny,[80] it happened that mention was made of the king of the English. In a pious declaration the abbot [Hugh] testified publicly, while many people listened, that during the previous night he had seen this same king accused before God's throne, and that he had received a sentence of damnation. Those listening were astonished, but when they con-

78. Anselm composed these two works between the summer of 1099 and the summer of 1100.

79. John 1.1.

80. The meeting between Anselm and Abbot Hugh of Cluny took place on 30 July 1100; Marcigny was a Cluniac convent of nuns. Hugh died in 1109 and was canonized in 1120.

sidered the eminence of the speaker, they could not but have faith in his words.

On the following day Anselm arrived at Lyons, and on the first of August, when all were sleeping, behold a young man in elegant attire and with a venerable expression appeared to the cleric who was lying before the door to Anselm's room, still awake as it seemed. Calling him by his name, the young man said: "Adam, are you sleeping?" "No," he answered, and the young man added: "Do you want to hear news?" "Gladly," Adam said, and the young man said: "Know for certain that the controversy between Archbishop Anselm and King William of England has been completely resolved." At this the cleric looked up and saw no one. The following night another cleric was standing with his eyes closed during the morning vigils and chanting the Psalms. Behold, a certain man showed him a document on which was written: "King William is dead." However, opening his eyes, he saw no one except his colleagues. And indeed at that very time in a dreadful manner the Lord executed his judgment on the impious king, and he who had lived like a beast met a bestial end. Anselm was sad, and just as Samuel mourned for Saul, who was cast down by the Lord,[81] so, sorrowful and distressed, he lamented that the king had provoked the wrath of the Lord against himself, for he would have preferred the king to be alive in the good graces of the Lord than dead in such a way.

Chapter Twelve

ANSELM RESTS IN THE MONASTERY OF LA CHAISE-DIEU AT THE TIME OF HIS FIRST EXILE. ON THE LIGHTNING AND THUNDER. ON THE DEATH OF KING WILLIAM II. ON KING HENRY. ON THE CASE EXAMINED BEFORE POPE PASCAL. ON THE FREEDOM OF CHRIST CHURCH, CANTERBURY.

81. 1 Samuel 15.35.

Three days later, when he was invited to and received honorably at a venerable place named La Chaise-Dieu,[82] he was resting at night. During a storm, lightning was flashing repeatedly on the mountain, and due to a great bolt of lightning, which caused fearful alarm, a great fire started in the barn where the monastery's hay was kept. The nearby buildings were engulfed, and there was dread and din. The smell of smoke was foul, and the bright blaze terrified everyone and scattered them in different directions. Hearing that the conflagration had increased, Father Anselm said, "Let us provide for ourselves, for 'It is your business when your neighbor's wall is on fire.'"[83] Going forth quickly, he came to the fire and made the sign of the life-giving cross over it. The fire subsided and, weakening, it left those buildings which it had attacked. And, what is more wondrous, although certain buildings in its path were consumed, the fire brought no harm to the hay of the monks who had the man of God as their guest.

Without delay Anselm returned to Lyons and received messengers from England announcing the death of the king and how the hand of the Lord had carried out a glorious vengeance for His Church. On the second day of August, which dawned after the vision at Lyons, this same king proceeded early in the morning to hunt in the woods which are called the New Forest by the inhabitants. There he was struck in the side by an arrow and, wounded in the heart, he expired. So in the same way while Basil was suffering, Julian was slain by a deadly weapon for the consolation of the Church,[84] so too, with a second Julian slain in England, Anselm was recalled for the consolation of the Church. Who shot either arrow is still uncertain. For Walter Tirel – who was accused by many of the king's death because he was a member of his household and was near him in chasing the wild beasts, and was almost the only one close by him even when he was at the point of death –

82. La Chaise-Dieu was a monastery in Auvergne, about seventy miles from Lyons.

83. Horace, *Epistles,* 1.18.84.

84. In the *Policraticus*, John devoted a long chapter (8.31) to the wretched end of all tyrants. He described the violent death of Julian, "the vile apostate and filthy emperor," in 360 when "God took pity on the prayers of the great Basil," the saintly bishop and doctor of the Church who died in 370.

testified, after invoking God's judgment on his own soul, that he had no part in the king's murder. There were many who claimed that the king himself had shot the arrow by which he was killed, and Walter constantly maintained this, although he was not believed. Certainly whoever did this faithfully obeyed the will of God, Who had pity on the misfortunes of His Church.

First of all, the monks of Canterbury rushed with all speed to their father. Then messengers of noblemen presented themselves in turn and expressed the devotion of the entire island. Moreover, Henry, the illustrious king of the English, who had succeeded his brother, faithfully arranged for the return of the archbishop, whom he had recalled.[85] He also promised that all the affairs of the kingdom would depend on Anselm's counsel. Indeed, at the beginning of his reign the king strove to be considered pious and gentle after the custom of rulers who are mild until they are firmly established. In fact, the condition of a realm is most calm under a new king. But when Anselm made known what had been done at the council in Rome to the new king at Salisbury [29 September 1100], the king was troubled, and everything turned to the contrary.

It would take a long time to report how many and how great were the sufferings Anselm endured for [the next] two years for the liberty of his churches. But when King Henry saw that Anselm's constancy was invincible, he proposed that Anselm go to Rome with the king's own emissaries and procure a remedy for the royal dignity that had been offended in England. All the bishops of England, along with abbots and noblemen, exclaimed that this proposal could not rightfully be denied the king. To this Archbishop Anselm said: "Since you wish it, I shall go, but the Church of God at Rome will do nothing at my advice or my request which would be injurious to the liberty of the churches, or which would dishonor the majesty of the apostolic see or my own integrity."

When the emissaries arrived at Rome with the archbishop [in October 1103], they were kindly received by Pope Pascal, who had succeeded Urban.[86] Then William, about whom we spoke above,

85. Henry I was crowned at Westminster on 5 August 1100, three days after the death of William II.

86. Pascal II was pope from 13 August 1099–21 January 1118.

set forth the king's case in his allotted time, and said among other things that the king would not allow investitures of churches to be taken away from him, not even if it meant the loss of his kingdom.[87] To this Pope Pascal responded: "If your king will not suffer to lose the investiture of churches, even if it means the loss of his kingdom, you should know and faithfully report to him as follows: Behold, before God I say that Pascal, even if it means ransoming his own life, will not permit the king to have these rights with impunity." And the [setting forth of] king's case was brought to an end in these terms.

How much Pascal granted to Anselm and bestowed upon him in his allotted time is clear from many examples, for he confirmed for him the primacy of Britain, which his predecessors had held from the time of Blessed Augustine.[88] He also personally granted this privilege: that Anselm would be exempt from the authority of all [papal] legates as long as he lived. Moreover, he compelled Gerard of York,[89] who was refusing to profess obedience to Anselm, to do so after his case was investigated (although when deceived, the pope sometimes wrote to the contrary.) He followed the decision in a case which was solemnly made and rendered in writing by Alexander, the Roman pontiff, in the time of Lanfranc.[90] Pascal's letters with their seals, which are still in the Church at Canterbury, make this known. What more? We do not recall that Pope Pascal rejected Anselm's petitions or deferred the wishes that he made known.

87. During Anselm's meeting with Henry I at Salisbury, the archbishop had reminded the king of the prohibition against lay investitures decreed at the Council at Rome in 1099.

88. Saint Augustine, "the Apostle of the English," was sent by Pope Gregory I to convert England in 596. As the first archbishop of Canterbury, he established the primacy of that see. He died in 604.

89. Gerard was archbishop of York. He died in 1108.

90. Pope Alexander II, a former pupil of Lanfranc's, supported his cause in the primacy conflict between Canterbury and York. See n100 below.

Chapter Thirteen

ANSELM AND HIS COMPANIONS REST FOR A NIGHT IN
FLORENCE. ON A CERTAIN MAN WHO LAY ON THE BED
OF SAINT ANSELM, AND WHAT HAPPENED TO HIM.
ON THE PROHIBITION OF SAINT ANSELM THE ARCH-
BISHOP FROM [ENTERING] THE KINGDOM OF ENGLAND
IN THE TIME OF HENRY THE FIRST. ON A CERTAIN BLIND
MAN RESTORED TO SIGHT BY SAINT ANSELM IN THE
TIME OF HIS SECOND EXILE. ON THE PEACE MADE
BETWEEN KING HENRY OF ENGLAND AND ANSELM.

As they were returning, they reached Florence, and there they
rested for one night. After they departed, the owner of the house
lay as usual on the bed in which Anselm had slept. While he was
sleeping, a man he did not know appeared and warned him to get
up from there quickly. And the man added that he was unworthy
to occupy the bed in which so great a guest had rested. When he
disregarded the warning, a more threatening and terrible vision
was repeated on the following night. When he was indeed dis-
turbed, but not to the point of yielding, it was made known on the
third night that he should rise quickly and stay away from there:
he would find out that what he was seeing was not a phantasm.
The man was terrified by his dream and went in the morning to
the bishop of the city. When he learned through him of Anselm's
holiness, he preserved his bed with all reverence from then on.

When they drew near to Lyons, and the often-named William
was about to depart from the archbishop, on behalf of the king of
England, he prohibited Anselm from entering England unless he
set aside his obedience to the apostolic see and promised that he
would faithfully observe all the customs of both King Williams [I
and II]. The archbishop was astonished at this, since he had left
[England] under other conditions. He remained at Lyons, and
upon William's return, King Henry ordered all Anselm's possessions confiscated.[91] Meanwhile, a certain blind man approached

91. Anselm resided at Lyons from November 1104–May 1105, then in Bec
until May 1106. During this period his possessions in England were confiscated.

Anselm in a chapel and obtained this favor: that he would make the sign of the cross with his thumb over the man's eyes. Anselm did this three times, saying: "May the power of Christ's cross give light to these eyes, drive all infirmity from them, and restore them to full health." And when he had sprinkled them with holy water, they were healed from blindness.

The king's displeasure, however, lasted for a year and a half. When certain ecclesiastical affairs demanded it, the man of God went to France [May–June 1105]. He was asked to proceed to Normandy by King Henry and at last received from the king the investiture of his property.[92] The king crossed over to England, and a few days later that William, who had so often harassed the archbishop as the kings' messenger, returned to Bec. On behalf of the king he asked very intently that, since all his earlier complaints had been laid to rest, Anselm visit England quickly. The bishop rejoiced over the liberty of the churches, which the mercy of God had now wrested from the kings.

Setting out on his journey, he came to Jumièges, where he was hindered by adverse health from proceeding any further and almost brought to his end by a lack of natural strength. Despair took hold of all his companions, and a swift and certain death seemed to stand at his door. During this time the father was urged for love of his sons to keep up his strength and allow some nourishment to be served to him. Though his words were halting and he was short of breath, he acknowledged that he had no appetite at all, was not even able [to eat]. Bishops and abbots gathered from all over so that they could plan for the passing away of that blessed spirit and see him off with psalms and hymns as he departed to Heaven. A certain member of his household, one of those serving in the monastery, while walking through the forest and not thinking about this matter, saw a little animal which they call a marten carrying a partridge in its mouth. He cried out and shook loose the partridge from the marten, which ran away. When the partridge was brought to Anselm, the sick man tasted it and, gaining

92. This refers to a "reinvestiture," or restoration, of Anselm's possessions. The meeting between him and the king took place on 22 July 1105.

strength contrary to expectation, he was a source of wonder and brought joy to all.

When those who had gathered were returning home, one of those serving [Abbot] Ralph of Séez[93] began to disparage Anselm greatly, asserting that one should not feel pity for someone who could have helped himself by taking nourishment if he had given up his display of vainglory. The abbot imposed silence on the man's recklessness, and a crowd of companions chided him on his immoderate language. He did not cease to abuse God's saint all the more ardently, in the manner of fools who do not accept words of wisdom. Persisting in such language as he hastily started on his journey, he ran with great force into a leafy oak tree in the forest through which his path lay. He fell off his horse with his foot held fast in one of the stirrups. When the horse became frightened, he was dragged here and there for a long time and violently shaken, so that he almost seemed to have breathed his last. But finally, after his companions called upon the Blessed Virgin, the horse was caught, and the wretched man, barely breathing, learned to spare the friends of God, since it is a very rash thing to make a judgment even about the servant of another.[94]

Chapter Fourteen

KING HENRY OF ENGLAND MADE A FRIENDLY VISIT
TO ARCHBISHOP ANSELM AT THE MONASTERY OF BEC
ON THE FEAST DAY OF BLESSED MARY'S ASSUMPTION.
ON A CLERIC WHO LOST HIS MIND. ON THE WAR
BETWEEN KING HENRY OF ENGLAND AND HIS BROTHER
ROBERT, THE COUNT OF NORMANDY. ANSELM WROTE
A LITTLE BOOK ENTITLED *ON THE HARMONY OF FORE-
KNOWLEDGE, PREDESTINATION AND THE GRACE OF GOD
WITH FREE WILL* IN ENGLAND. ON THE ELECTION
OF THOMAS OF YORK.

93. Ralph later became bishop of Rochester, 1108–1111, and then arch-bishop of Canterbury from 1114–1122.
94. Romans 14.4.

King Henry returned to Normandy and made a friendly visit to the archbishop at Bec on the feast of the assumption of the Blessed Virgin Mary [15 August 1106]. At about that time Anselm consecrated a chapel for the courtyard at the request of the abbot and with the approval of the archbishop of Rouen. During this consecration by his blessing alone he restored a cleric suffering from the loss of his mind to his former health.

This man [Anselm] who had been an exile and long-afflicted by insults for God's sake and who had made the circuit of the sees of others thereafter, with God triumphing over men, as is just, returned with honor and glory to his own [September 1106]. There a rich English nobleman stricken with a serious bodily infirmity sent messengers to ask for bread blessed by him, and receiving it, he was cured by it according to his faith. Meanwhile, the king, who was spending time in Normandy, rejoiced over the peace and could not keep secret his confidence that the Lord was favorably disposed to him over the fact that he had accepted Anselm as his friend in true and steadfast friendship. Hence he promised himself [that he would conquer] the whole of Normandy in a short time, and indeed not in vain, for after battle was joined, he defeated and captured his brother and his supporters.[95] After he achieved this victory, he wrote a letter to Anselm in which he ascribed it to the merits of the concord and peace which had been re-established between them.

Furthermore, when the king and the archbishop met together on August first [1107 at Winchester], the triumph of the Church was clear to all. The king openly yielded and granted the investiture of churches to the archbishop, neither did he demand any payment of homage in [episcopal] elections except what was agreed upon and was such that the sacred canons did not prevent.[96] By not assuming for himself the right to choose or to invest with the crosier according to ancient custom, the king allowed

95. Henry I was victorious in the Battle of Tinchebrai on 28 September 1106.

96. John of Salisbury is correct here in reporting the concessions made by Henry I, but in return the prohibition against homage by bishops and abbots was withdrawn. Thus, this settlement was more a compromise than a total triumph for Anselm.

canonical decisions to go forward in the disposition of churches. Meanwhile, the servant of God wrote one little book, *On the Harmony of Foreknowledge, Predestination and God's Grace with Free Will*,[97] on which he delayed, contrary to custom, because he was so infirm of body that he did not go from place to place on horseback from then on, but was always carried in a litter.

So as Anselm's end approached, the younger Thomas of York was chosen [archbishop][98] and, under Anselm's orders, ordained a priest by William, the bishop of Winchester,[99] and he began to press on with disputes between the churches of Canterbury and York that had been brought to an end.[100] Anselm, although extremely weak in body, but endowed with strength from on high, commanded the individual bishops of all of England by virtue of the obedience owed him not to have dealings with Thomas until he desisted from the rebellion he had begun. He also directed that the letters patent with his seal, by which this was ordered, be very carefully preserved in all the dioceses of the bishops. Determined on this point, he also sent a letter to Thomas in these words.

Chapter Fifteen

THE LETTER OF SAINT ANSELM[101] AS HE LAY LANGUISHING IN HIS BED TO THOMAS, [ARCHBISHOP] ELECT OF YORK, CONCERNING THE JURISDICTION OF CHRIST CHURCH, CANTERBURY.

"Anselm, servant of the Church at Canterbury, to Thomas, archbishop elect of York.

97. This work was composed in 1107/1108.
98. Thomas was archbishop of York from 1109–1114.
99. William Giffard was bishop of Winchester from 1100–1129.
100. From the time of Lanfranc, the first Norman archbishop, a protracted dispute over ecclesiastical primacy in the British Isles was carried on by the archbishops of Canterbury and York. Pope Pascal II ordered archbishop Gerard of York to profess obedience to Anselm (see ch. 12 above), but now Thomas, as archbishop-elect, was resuming the conflict.
101. Letter no. 472, dated to March or April 1109; cf. *The Letters of St. Anselm*, ed. Walter Frölich (Kalamazoo, MI, 1993) 3: 265–266.

"I, Anselm, in the sight of Almighty God, archbishop of Canterbury and primate of the whole of Britain, say to you, Thomas, speaking on behalf of God Himself, that I forbid you the use of the priestly office which you received by my order in my diocese through my suffragan bishop, and I command you not to presume in any way to involve yourself in any pastoral care until you desist from the rebellion which you have undertaken against the Church at Canterbury, and until you declare publicly your subjection to it (which your predecessors, namely archbishops Thomas and Gerard, professed according to the ancient custom of their predecessors). But if you choose to persist in these ways which you have begun rather than to desist from them, I interdict all the bishops in the whole of Britain, under the pain of perpetual excommunication, so that none of them might lay their hands on you to ordain you to the bishopric, or if you should be ordained by foreign bishops, that none will accept you as a bishop or in any Christian community. On God's behalf I forbid you also, Thomas, under the same pain of excommunication, to ever accept consecration to the bishopric of York unless you make the profession (which your predecessors Thomas and Gerard made to the Church at Canterbury). But if you renounce the bishopric of York altogether, I grant that you may use the priestly office which you have already received."

As he used to say when asked, Anselm was afraid to appear in the sight of God his judge unless he had first punished such great disobedience arising in his time in the jurisdiction entrusted to him. Thus this same Thomas, frightened by the authority of the man and the severity of the sentence, came to his senses and made his profession before the suffragan bishops of the Church of Canterbury who were present in place of the primate after Anselm's death.[102]

---

102. Anselm died on 21 April 1109; Thomas made his profession and was consecrated in that year.

Chapter Sixteen

ANSELM BEGINS HIS LITTLE BOOK *ON THE ORIGIN
OF THE SOUL*. HE DOES NOT FINISH IT BECAUSE HE
IS PREVENTED BY DEATH. ON THE DEATH OF ANSELM
ON APRIL 21ST AND IN THE [16TH] YEAR OF HIS BISHOP-
RIC. ON THE BALSAM THAT WAS AUGMENTED
AND ON ANSELM'S MIRACLES.

And so, in the third year after Anselm was recalled by King Henry from his second exile [1109], he began to be so weakened that all food was distasteful to him. Yet, he kept up his strength by taking in food because he knew that his strength could not last without nourishment. His flesh became more and more infirm, but that magnanimous and noble spirit, in its love of God, scorned its infirmity for the Church. Indeed, he seemed stronger and more fit because of it, neither could he be kept from meditations and religious discussions and prayers, but was constantly engaged in his customary practices that were pleasing to God. He was present daily at the consecration of the Lord's body, going there either on foot or carried in a chair. He could barely be kept from there on the fifth day before his death.

Palm Sunday dawned and one of those who were present addressed him thus: "Father, it is very likely from what we observe that you will leave this world and pass on to the Easter feast of your Lord." And he said: "According to His will, so be it. And may the Lord's pleasure concerning me be fulfilled as He wills. But if He would prefer, I would wish the investigation into the origin of the soul, which I am turning over in my mind, to be faithfully completed before my death." He did not feel any pain in his body, and on account of this he was truly failing as his stomach was weakening. Then toward evening on Tuesday, although he now barely formed his words, he blessed those present, the king, queen, their children and all their subjects at the request of Ralph, bishop of Rochester,[103] and he absolved them as far as it was in his power.

---

103. I.e. Ralph of Séez, mentioned above (ch. 13).

At Lauds the brothers were present at the Church of the Savior, and one of those standing by him began the Lord's Passion. When he came to the words of the Lord Jesus, "You are the ones who have remained with me in my trials, and I bestow on you a kingdom, just as my Father has bestowed a kingdom on me, that you might eat and drink at my table in my kingdom,"[104] Anselm, drawing breath more slowly than usual and now near the end, was placed in ashes and sackcloth. With the brothers gathered around him, as much as their sorrow and tears permitted, he fell asleep in the Lord.[105]

He passed away in the brightening dawn of the Wednesday preceding Our Lord's Supper, which was the 21st of April in the year of the Lord's Incarnation 1109, the sixteenth year of his bishopric and the seventy-sixth of his life. His blessed passing and glorious translation [to heaven] were proclaimed by miraculous signs; and the confessor's most holy merits became known openly from the visible miracles there. Venerable men, namely the above-mentioned bishop of Rochester and Baldwin, whom the holy man had made steward of his affairs, as we said, were employed in anointing the holy countenance with the little balsam which they had. The bishop, as he was about to perform this duty, drew forth his finger from the bottom of the vessel. It was barely covered at the tip, and he saw that the balsam had altogether run out since the vessel had been carelessly maintained. He was troubled, and all present were saddened. A respected man whom we mentioned at the beginning, Eadmer, asked the bishop to turn the vessel over and shake it vigorously into his hand. The bishop assented and behold, from the almost dry vessel liquid flowed in abundance and filled the open hand below. This was done a second and third time and repeated even more often, and the vessel always flowed abundantly. With tears bursting forth for joy and wonder, those who were present repeatedly took turns to anoint the holy man's entire body thoroughly. For why, in light of God's great bounty, would they allow themselves to be accused of stinginess or avarice?

104. Luke 22.28–30.
105. Acts 7.60.

When Elias was supplying oil it was multiplied,[106] so too the balsam was increased to accommodate Anselm. Indeed, it was a worthy thing that the flesh which he strove to keep uncorrupted by pleasures while living should not experience the harm of corruption after death.

When Father Anselm was dying, a certain man, a true follower of Christ and the Church, and a succorer of the poor according to his means, had come to the hour of his death, as it seemed, at Canterbury. Indeed, he had languished for a long time. When he had drifted off for a moment into a light sleep, a handsome youth appeared and asked what he was suffering. He said: "See, I am dying." The youth said to him: "The father of our country, who is about to live forever, now goes to God, and you are dying? Arise quickly and glorify God and his friend, Father Anselm, who comes to your assistance." After he heard these words, the man rose up to the astonishment of all, and moved to give thanks, he proceeded to the church and revealed what he had seen.

Also at the hour of his passing, a brother in the monastery of Blessed Augustine, concerned about the status of the glorious father, saw in a vision a most beautiful band of persons clothed in white at the door to the archbishop's room as if waiting with longing for the arrival of someone about to come out. Presiding over that multitude was a bishop, distinguished by his habit and by a certain majesty, who was coming in and going out. At Anselm's death, he came forth in haste and said: "Behold, he whom you are expecting is here! Receive him, and take him with words of praise and exultation where the Lord has commanded."

A few days earlier, a certain monk of the Church at Canterbury, Elias by name, an innocent man and one of an approved way of life, saw the passing of Father Anselm in another vision. It seemed to him that he saw most Blessed Dunstan[107] and Archbishop Anselm conversing together in Christ Church, and that he heard these words spoken by Dunstan to Anselm: "Dearest friend, take this little ring in your hand; may you be willing to accept it."

106. 3 Kings 17.16.
107. Saint Dunstan, a Benedictine monk, was archbishop of Canterbury from 960–988.

Drawing back his hand, Blessed Dunstan said: "Not this time; I am keeping it for a while. On the Wednesday before Easter you will receive it from the hand of the Lord." So in fact was the passing of Martin made known in a vision to the saints,[108] and the Lord, Whom they served in like ways, glorified Martin and Anselm in an equal manner.

Chapter Seventeen

ON THE MIRACLES OF SAINT ANSELM, ARCHBISHOP OF CANTERBURY, AFTER HIS DEATH. ON THE COFFIN IN WHICH HIS BODY WAS ENCLOSED. ON THE BISHOP OF ROCHESTER'S CHAPLAIN, AND ON COUNT ARNULF IN TROUBLE AT SEA.

After these things were done which religious custom demanded, it remained to enclose that precious treasure of his body in a tomb. And so they went to the coffin, and it was found to be too small to receive the body unless the limbs were broken and the upper stone was removed. Since this seemed too harsh and intolerable to all, one of the brothers who were standing around seized the bishop's crosier and approached the stone; he drew the crosier along all the sides and pressed it in such a way, adjusting it here and there, so that, to the wonder of all, the coffin seemed very suitable and sufficient for receiving the body. For the Savior, at whose passing the rocks were split,[109] did this for His own glory, so that the nature of stone might be seen to yield wondrously to His confessor.

In those days, while crossing a bridge in London, a certain chaplain of the bishop of Rochester named Robert, a monk by profession and one praiseworthy for his reputation for good morals, sensed that the protection of Blessed Father Anselm was sustaining him, and he was glad, for the horse which was carrying his

---

108. Just as in chapter 4 above, John's source for the vision at the death of Saint Martin is Gregory of Tours' *The Miracles of Saint Martin* (1.5).

109. Matthew 27.51.

servant and pack fell into the Thames River, without the servant but weighed down by packages. Although the poor man could be troubled over the loss of his horse and possessions, yet nothing distressed his mind except one of the books of Anselm, which he believed had been placed in the pack, and he grieved that it was lost. But it turned out otherwise, for when, after often invoking Father Anselm, the chaplain reached the riverbank, he found the horse, the pack with its little bundles, the book too and everything that he had lost, unharmed.

Count Arnulf, the son of Roger of Montgomery, was returning to England from Normandy;[110] at first he sailed halfway across the sea with the wind favoring his voyage. When the wind failed, the oarsmen were disheartened, and two whole days later after provisions ran out, they suffered shipwreck from the instability and uncertainty of the winds. At last the count turned to Blessed Anselm. He asked his companions and sailors to entrust the entire ship to Blessed Anselm, whom they had known, and of whose sanctity they had no doubt for he, who was ever merciful while his mortal body detained him, had promised that he would not desert suppliants, since, now newly joined to God and hindered by no obstacle, he would be inflamed with even greater charity. All agreed. They had scarcely completed the Lord's Prayer with this intention, and behold, the dark clouds dissipated, and they were brought by a favoring wind to England, where they wanted to go. Coming to the king's court, they reported to the king and others what had happened to them, and they loosened the tongues of all who heard them in praise of the illustrious confessor.

To these examples [we add this]: one of the brothers at Canterbury was very concerned about the status of Father Anselm. He prayed to the Lord that He might make him more certain of this. Therefore, Anselm appeared to his friend in a vision admonishing him to be certain, because from the moment when he was free from the burden of flesh, Jesus Christ, Whom he had truly worshipped, received him in glory and placed on him the stole of immortality.

---

110. Arnulf was the son of Roger, earl of Shrewsbury, who died in 1094.

Chapter Eighteen

ON THE MIRACLES OF OUR HOLY FATHER ANSELM,
ARCHBISHOP OF CANTERBURY. ON A CERTAIN MONK
OF CHRIST CHURCH AT CANTERBURY WHO APPROACHED
THE TOMB OF OUR HOLY FATHER ANSELM TO PRAY,
EITHER TO ANSELM OR FOR ANSELM; HE WAS
WORTHY OF BEING PRAYED TO AS A SAINT BECAUSE
HIS NAME IS WRITTEN IN THE BOOK OF LIFE.
AND ON HIS OTHER MIRACLES.

It will be a long book if all the things of this kind which happened then are reported. But, since we have promised succinct brevity, let this book be concluded in a few words, and let those who wish to know more have recourse to the sources. I am speaking of the vast volumes from which these accounts have been taken with such great moderation, as it were, for the consolation and refreshment of those traveling [on the path of life].

A certain monk of the Church at Canterbury, a novice, was moved by his devotion and among others who were going in multitudes to the tomb of Father Anselm went there to pray. Yet, he was in doubt about what manner of prayer would be better, namely to Anselm or for Anselm. When he was uneasy for a long time in vacillation of this kind, he turned with complete devotion to the Lord, asking that he might be instructed on what he ought to do. And since he often invoked our blessed Lord with integrity, in a vision a book was opened for him where he was praying before the altar; in this book was most fittingly written: "Saint Anselm." And so that devout man understood that Anselm's name was written in the Book of Life, and by the merits of his preceding life he was worthy to be entreated as a saint.

Another brother in the same church was stricken by a serious illness and languished for a long time, and he did not know at all where to turn for help. But afterward he turned with complete devotion to the well-known compassion of Saint Anselm. He was brought to Anselm's tomb and, prostrate on the ground,[111] he

---

111. *humi fusus* echoes Vergil, *Aeneid* 1.193.

prayed intently that the Church might be relieved of its burden either by his cure or by his death. The Most High heard his heart's desire,[112] and the one who had called upon Anselm was restored to health.

A nobleman named Humphrey, a knight who was upright and known to many, suffered from dropsy and was abandoned by all his physicians out of despair. This man had loved Anselm, and was not able to let him fade from his memory. Therefore, he asked a monk of Canterbury named Haimo, who had been known to him from of old, to come to him so that he might take counsel for his soul. Haimo came, and by chance brought with him the cincture of Blessed Anselm. The knight warmly kissed this and, after a prayer was said first, he strove to wrap it around himself. However, the ends were barely able to touch each other because of his swelling. But truly, in a wondrous way, his body began gradually to cease swelling and to return to its natural state. Sensing this, the knight wrapped the cincture around all his limbs, and to the glory of the most holy confessor, he was restored to perfect health.

In Lyons, near Saint Irenaeus [monastery], a certain very religious recluse saw herself led on a certain night to the throne of the ever-Virgin, where, when she had heard and seen many wondrous proclamations of the heavenly homeland, she asked among other things what should be expected concerning Hugh, the archbishop of Lyons.[113] The Virgin Mother said: "It will be well for him, daughter, well through the grace of God." And the recluse added: "O my Lady Queen, what may I know about my lord Anselm, archbishop of Canterbury?" Our Lady said to her: "Concerning him you may be most assured that he is without doubt in the great glory of God."

One of those who had been a member of his household saw a similar vision in England at almost the same time. For he saw Father Anselm clothed in white and arrayed in his pontifical vestments. Recalling that Anselm was freed from human affairs, he said: "Where do you dwell, Father? How do you live? What do you

112. Psalm 20.2.
113. Archbishop Hugh of Lyons had welcomed Anselm with hospitality during his exiles. He died on 7 October 1106.

do?" And Anselm responded: "I live there, where I see, I rejoice and I enjoy." When the man awoke, he reflected upon these things and grieved that one of the four verbs had escaped him. In his sadness he heard during a certain brief sleep a voice saying clearly to him "I rejoice," and this was in fact the word he had let slip from his mind. Made even more certain of Father Anselm's glory as a result of this, he exulted all the more, and gave great thanks to the Creator.

In order that the glory of the blessed confessor might extend to foreigners, a certain matron born of English nobility in the region of Scotland and approved in every way in the Christian religion, Estrylde by name, was brought to the point of death by a serious illness. Eventually she regained her health completely after she was girded with the cincture of Blessed Anselm, about which we have already spoken. Eadmer, a man worthy of pleasing remembrance, was present at these events; he observed them and recorded them.

In the Church at Canterbury a sick brother was afflicted by a violent fever. When all the aid of physicians had come to naught, Eadmer took care to encircle his neck with the cincture we have spoken about, and he was cured. It is not expedient to report how many women in labor also were aided in childbirth by this cincture, since it is a very long list and known to many. A brother who had a huge tumor like a large ball growing under his navel was cured by this same cincture without any rupture. The Church at Canterbury has acknowledged this because what was done is renowned there.

It is commonly known that a certain Elphege was blind, deaf, dumb and lame from birth. Indeed, this is commonly known. This man, as the present day bears witness, recovered full health in all these senses at the tomb of Blessed Anselm.

A conflagration took hold of a certain street of [Bury] St. Edmund's [and] the house of a certain man who had been a pupil of Blessed Anselm, and who owned nothing else.[114] The devouring

114. The date is uncertain, but Southern (*The Life*, p. 169) concludes that this incident took place in 1123 or 1124.

fire,[115] which consumed everything, had already invaded his house. There was no solace for the man, when, behold, a brother advised him to remember Anselm, his teacher, and entrust the house to him who was accustomed to extinguish flames. The man obeyed, and before he even finished the Lord's Prayer, he marveled and rejoiced that his house was saved from the conflagration without harm. Elias, the venerable abbot of La-Trinité-du-Mont in Rouen, admitted openly that through the prayers and merits of Blessed Anselm, when he was ordained by him, he had been cured of a swelling and pain in his knees with which he was so tormented that he could scarcely walk.[116]

But who am I to expound on the righteousness of the Lord, and to touch on the praises of so great a father with my presumptuous mouth or pen? To describe so great a confessor worthily exceeds my strength and my worth; to describe him improperly is a sign of presumption, a matter rightly and deservedly subject to punishment. But may Father Anselm be gracious to me, and by his merits and prayers may he direct my mind to useful and upright employment, and to what is pleasing to the Divine Majesty. Also, I beseech the listener and reader, and I implore them by whatever supplication is permitted, that they might solicit holy Father Anselm with me and for me, and that they might obtain for me and for themselves pardon for their transgressions from Him Who alone is blessed forever. Amen.

115. *ignis edax* echoes Vergil, *Aeneid,* 2.758.
116. Elias was abbot there from 1120–1130.

The Life of Thomas Becket

HERE BEGINS THE PROLOGUE
TO THE LIFE OF SAINT THOMAS THE MARTYR
BY MASTER JOHN OF SALISBURY.

The Ancient Enemy fights continually against the most holy Church, but the Son of God, who redeemed it with His own blood, defends it by the blood of His members and carries it forward to true freedom. Preeminent among these members are the glorious band of apostles[1] and the host of holy martyrs clothed in purple. Made firm by their teaching, made strong by their example, made solid by their blood as if by a certain cement and glue, as it were, are the living stones in the building of Christ's body, so that the Church, advancing, may be extended and grow in the number of the faithful and in virtue into a holy temple in the Lord.[2] Although all martyrs have a special claim on everlasting glory, yet the honor is more illustrious and the crown shines more brightly than the rest for those who, deserving because of a double dignity, perform the office of teachers, made truly a model to their flock,[3] and who in the time of need lay down their life for their sheep.[4] For just as star differs from star in brightness, so at the resurrection of the saints, the righteous, each in their own order, will shine like constellations, and those who guide many toward [eternal] life by their teaching will be like the splendor of the firmament for all eternity.[5]

1. Cf. *Te Deum*, l. 13.
2. Ephesians 2.21.
3. 1 Peter 5.3.
4. John 10.15.
5. Daniel 12.3.

To these must Saint Thomas, the archbishop of Canterbury, be rightly and deservedly joined, so that he who lived as a sharer of tribulation and suffering for Christ might be co-heir with them of consolation and glory in Him. So that his merits might shine forth more brightly, let this concise and quite brief discourse review the sum of his way of life. For if perchance it is someone's wish to know the whole sequence of his deeds, this will have to be obtained from the vast volumes which have been written by him and about him, so that it might stand as a commendation of God's grace, which inspires where it wills,[6] how in a brief time in various occupations he filled many seasons.[7] His letters indicate this, and the writings of others, full of credibility and worthy to repeat, which, if they are examined diligently, will be able to encourage both present and future generations to virtue.

HERE THE PROLOGUE ENDS.

HERE BEGINS THE LIFE AND SUFFERING
OF SAINT THOMAS THE MARTYR.

1. The aforementioned most-blessed Thomas, a native of the city of London, illustrious offspring of modest parents, was endowed with manifold graces from the first years of his youth. Indeed, he was tall in stature, handsome in appearance, acute in intellect, pleasant and agreeable in speech, amiable for his age in the beauty of his ways, and he possessed such great keenness of reason that he wisely solved unusual and difficult questions. And he was blessed with so fertile a memory that what he had once learned through pronouncements or conversations, he could cite without difficulty almost as often as he wished. Many more-scholarly men who were not able to achieve this used to ascribe so great a liveliness of mind to a miracle, especially in a man given to diverse preoccupations. In fact, a nourishing grace so attended the future bishop that in

6. John 3.8.
7. Wisdom 4.13.

conferences or in the course of speech it provided him with all he needed right at hand, as we say.

2. Moreover, from early youth, as he used to say, he learned fear of the Lord from his mother, and to invoke with delight the Blessed Virgin as the guide of his ways and patron of his life, and to cast his whole trust upon her after Christ. With full compassion he used to have pity on those who beg in public, and he aided them with such effect that he could say with Blessed Job, "From the beginning mercy took root in me, and dutiful love came forth with me from my mother's womb."[8]

3. Upon leaving the schools of liberal studies, he turned his attention to the business of the courts, and in their serious matters and their trifles, just as the spirit moved him, he quickly prevailed. And so he easily surpassed his comrades and contemporaries. Moreover, although he was governed by youthful inclinations, as the goads of age impel us, yet zeal for the faith and nobility of spirit were thriving in him. However, he was one who excessively "courted the popular breeze,"[9] and what we read about Saint Brice of Tours[10] should be affirmed, I have no doubt, about him: that although he was proud and vain, and sometimes assumed the appearance and put forth the words of those who love foolishly, yet he must be admired and imitated for his bodily chastity.

4. But when he saw that many things were carried out in the courts of nobles against the integrity of the clergy, and that his association with them was perniciously opposed to the purpose to which he was dedicated, through the inspiration and guidance of grace rather than the counsel or intervention of friends, he betook himself to Archbishop Theobald of Canterbury, that father of blessed memory, [11] and because of his meritorious diligence, in a short time he was found worthy to be enrolled among the very few in the archbishop's immediate household. How many and how great the exertions he undertook there for the Church of God, how

8. Job 31.18 slightly altered.
9. Livy 3.33.7.
10. See Introduction, p. 13.
11. A former abbot of Bec, Theobald was archbishop of Canterbury from 1138–1161.

often he visited the papal curia[12] to facilitate ecclesiastical interests, with how happy an outcome he expedited the tasks that were enjoined upon him, it is in no way easy to tell, especially in a short account that does not describe individual acts, but that assembles the sum of events and strives to set forth the reason for his martyrdom.

5. In order that an ability in pleading and deciding cases, and in teaching people might be furnished to the bishop predestined by God, he devoted himself to the study of civil law and sacred canons. And so that through his experience of affairs he might more easily attain familiarity with church stewardship, he was appointed archdeacon of the holy Church at Canterbury [October 1154], at whose bosom he had been nurtured, by the aforementioned archbishop.

6. After a short interval of time, when Henry, duke of Normandy and Aquitaine, the son of Count Geoffrey of Anjou and the Empress Matilda, had succeeded King Stephen in the kingdom of England,[13] it was arranged by the forenamed archbishop that his archdeacon might be made chancellor of the realm. For the young age of the king was suspect to the archbishop, and he feared the foolishness and malice of the youths and perverse men by whose advice the king seemed to be guided. And so that the king might not, through their instigation, act more insolently to subject the people by his rights as a conqueror, which he seemed to himself [to be] (although it was otherwise), the archbishop arranged for Thomas to be appointed chancellor to the court in order that through his aid and support he might restrain the violent impulse of the new king lest he vent his rage upon the Church; also that the chancellor might temper the maliciousness of the advice given to the king, and repress the boldness of officials who, under the guise of public authority and the pretext of law, conspired to plunder the property of the Church and of the provincial bishops.

12. *Apostolorum limina*: literally, "threshold of the apostles."
13. Stephen died in October 1154, and Henry II was crowned king of England on 19 December of that year. Becket was appointed chancellor in late December 1154 or early January 1155.

7. However, at the beginning of his chancellorship he endured so many and such great scarcities of various necessities; he was worn down by so many hardships; he was almost overwhelmed by so many afflictions, threatened by so many ambushes, exposed to so many snares at court from the malice of those who dwelt there, that often from day to day he grew weary of living, as he was wont to tell his archbishop and friends, with tears as his witness, and that, after his longing for eternal life, he wished above all that he could, without the stigma of disgrace, be extricated from the obligations of the court. For although the world in all its flatteries seemed to fawn on him and to applaud him, he was not unmindful of his position or his burden: on one side for the safety and honor of his lord, the king, and on the other side for the needs of the Church and the provincial bishops, he was forced to struggle daily as much against the king himself as against the king's enemies, and by various stratagems to elude various wicked deceptions. But this especially he pointed out repeatedly: that he had to fight without ceasing against the beasts of the court, and to carry on business with Proteus,[14] as we say, and to be trained in wrestling, as it were.[15] For almost at every breeze, ruin and a headlong fall threatened him, except that grace and diligence preserved him.

8. Nevertheless, while performing the duties of chancellor in the king's palace, he found such great favor in his eyes that, after the death of the forenamed archbishop of Canterbury, the king arranged that he be set over the primary see of Britain, so that the king might more easily rule the whole English Church. Having tested his magnanimity and loyalty in many matters, the king believed that he was well-suited for such an exalted rank; that he could easily be inclined toward the king's service; that he would manage everything in ecclesiastical and secular affairs according to the king's will; moreover, if an untimely death should cut short the king's days, he was providing a most faithful tutor for his heirs. Being a most experienced man, however, and well accustomed (more than can readily be said) to judge the future, Thomas

14. Cf. Horace, *Satires*, 2.3.71. Proteus was a sea god who could change his shape at will.
15. Cf. Vergil, *Aeneid*, 6.642.

weighed keenly enough the peril of so great a charge. He had
learned by lengthy experience what difficulty that see might hold,
and what glory. Also, he knew the king's ways, as well as the de-
pravity and obstinacy of his officials, and how efficient was the
malice of informers in that court. From these circumstances he
concluded very correctly that if he undertook the proffered office,
he would lose the favor of God or of the king. For he could not
cling to God[16] while complying with the impulses of the king, nor
could he fail to have the king as an enemy while preferring the
laws of the saints to him.

9. So for some time he struggled against the king and others
who wanted him to be promoted, but the divine election prevailed
so that, when the venerable Henry of Pisa, cardinal-priest and
legate of the apostolic see,[17] urged and persuaded and earnestly
encouraged him, he assented to the wish of the king and the counsel of his friends [spring 1162]. He preferred to be in peril with
the king rather than that the see be vacant any longer while the
Church was subject to many dangers. In his heart he determined
firmly either to free the Church from the wretchedness of so great
a servitude or, in imitation of Christ, to lay down his life for his
sheep.[18] For the public authority, taking away the privilege of the
Church, was restoring to its own scrutiny all cases indifferently,
the ecclesiastical ones as well as the secular, and just as the people
were being trampled on, so also was the priest.[19]

10. Therefore, although certain of his rivals in particular,[20]
against the counsel of the Divine Will, tried to impede the promo-

16. Psalm 72.28
17. Henry of Pisa was one of Pope Alexander III's two legates in France.
He supported Becket's nomination to the archbishopric and counseled him to
accept it.
18. John 10.15.
19. John likely alludes here to the question of "criminous clerks," i.e., to
the trial of all clergy in ecclesiastical courts in both civil and criminal cases.
King Henry II increasingly opposed this principle and its abuses, some of
which were quite flagrant examples of injustice and extreme leniency. The
issue became a major point of conflict between the king and the archbishop.
20. Although there was surely opposition to Becket's election, the only
voice publicly raised against it was that of Gilbert Foliot, bishop of Hereford,
who later became bishop of London.

tion of him whom God had chosen for Himself to be a future bishop and martyr, he was unanimously elected by all.[21]

11. After he was consecrated, he immediately "put off the old man"[22] and put on the hair shirt and the monk, crucifying his flesh along with his vices and concupiscences.[23] Recalling also that he had received the office of teacher and pastor, he fulfilled the duty of preaching, almost always devoting to prayer and reading whatever time he could take away from more pressing affairs. While celebrating Mass alone, he used to be drenched in tears to a wondrous degree, and he so conducted himself in the office of the altar as if he saw the Lord's Passion carried out in actual presence in his flesh. He handled the divine sacraments most reverently, so that his very touching of them might instruct the faith and morals of those looking on. He kept his hands away from every gift, and absolutely banished the filth of avarice from his household. He was also prudent in counsels, both a diligent and discreet listener in the airing of cases, subtle in interrogations, ready in refutations, just in judgments and, absolutely impartial, a most righteous administrator of the law in all matters. Lest vainglory diminish his merits, he carefully concealed the soldier of Christ[24] under the beauty of his vesture, so that his appearance might be agreeable to the people, according to the edict of a wise man, though inwardly almost everything would be different.[25] He did not proceed into his palace to his table unless he was preceded by paupers, and he wanted the table richly and refreshingly made grand for this purpose, so that from what was leftover he might more fully and pleasingly comfort the needy. None of the beggars going door to door went away empty from his gates. He used to have his followers search out the hearths of the sick and feeble with diligence, and he visited them with kindness, supporting very many of them with daily nourishment and clothing. As a matter of fact, al-

21. Becket was elected on 23 May 1162 and consecrated archbishop of Canterbury on 2 June 1162.

22. Colossians 3.9.

23. Galatians 5.24. For the significance of "putting on the monk" see above, pp. 13–14.

24. 2 Timothy 2.3.

25. Seneca, *Moral Epistles to Lucilius*, 5.3.

though Theobald, his predecessor of pious memory, had been accustomed to double the amount of alms established by his own
predecessors, he thought in his religious zeal that even Theobald's
double ought to be doubled. He devoted a tenth of all which he
collected from any title to the observance of this charitable work.
In his private little chapel every day on bended knees he used to
wash the feet of thirteen paupers in memory of Christ, bestowing
on each of them, after they were fully refreshed by food, four silver
coins. But if by chance at some time, though rarely, he was
prevented from doing this personally, he saw to it that it was very
diligently carried out by a deputy. He received men from the religious orders with such great reverence that he could be thought to
venerate in them the divine presence, or angels. He so excelled in
practicing hospitality and other works of generosity that whatever
goods were among his possessions could be thought to be the common patrimony of all. And although his household was renowned
for opulent furnishings and various trappings of business in
accordance with the custom of his people, yet, for Christ, the
riches and wealth and every ornament of the world he despised as
dung.[26] He used transitory goods to provide for necessities rather
than enjoying them to satisfy the pleasures of desire. In food and
drink he observed moderation, so that he might not be accused of
scrupulosity by abstaining absolutely, nor be burdened by intoxi-
cation for consuming these immoderately. In fact, avoiding almost
equally the mark of a guilty person and of a hypocrite, he judged
that kind of fasting to be best: to preserve a degree of moderation.
And indeed, wearing lavish garments, he was a pauper in spirit;
outwardly happy, he was contrite of heart; choosing abstemi-
ousness at a sumptuous table, he sometimes had a stomach more
empty than refreshed, and he was more often revived than full.
Remaining always sober, he adapted himself to those whom he
lived with, following the Apostle who, with most salutary stewardship, became all things to all men so that he might win over
all.[27] He used to set the pauper free from the mighty[28] as one who

26. Philippians 3.8.
27. 1 Corinthians 9.22.
28. Psalm 72.11.

was truly given by the Lord to be a father of the poor and a consoler of the grieving. He freely censured the vices of any powerful officials, knowing that where the Spirit of the Lord is, consequently there also is freedom.[29] Yet, being a discreet man, he used to weigh the morals of men whom he censured or warned, so that he might not bestow a holy thing on dogs or cast pearls before swine.[30] And since a heavenly anointing was guiding him, whether he conversed with literate or illiterate men, he appeared wondrously erudite and eloquent, and his preaching was pleasing and efficacious as much for the weight of his opinions as for the purity of his words. Furthermore, after banquets and sleep exacted when necessity demanded, once again over and above his day's work, he devoted himself to business or writing or worthy studies and conversations, fleeing leisure with utmost effort, so that his enemies might not see him and deride his days of rest.[31] Moreover, what he could subtract from his nightly sleep without serious harm to his body, he gave over to tears and prayers and holy meditations, striving after chastity of body, preserving virtue in his heart, modesty in speech, justice in his actions, so that by the example of his own holiness he might more effectually inspire those whom he was about to instruct by his words. He fought tirelessly against heretics and schismatics, and he could never be induced to have dealings with excommunicated persons. Whoever was opposed to sound doctrine, he did not doubt would be his enemy in Christ. Burning with zeal for justice also, he strove to preserve for every person what was his own, without showing any favoritism or accepting any bribes whatsoever.

12. The Ancient Enemy, seeing that so great a man would very much benefit the Church of God, looked with malice upon him and, lest the land should enjoy a hoped-for peace any longer, he chose many mighty inciters of discord through whom he sowed seeds of hatred in the heart of the king and his courtiers. Since a dispute had arisen over the customs of the realm and ecclesiastical

29. 2 Corinthians 3.17.
30. Matthew 7.6.
31. Lamentations 1.7.

authority,[32] which these men provoked, he incited the sons of perdition,[33] who were trying to subvert the freedom of the Church, to destroy the holy man. But although all [churches] were oppressed, the Church at Canterbury distressed him [Becket] more. Its power, honor and service were diminished as, first, Roger, archbishop of York,[34] and then many of the magnates rose up against it, even those who were obliged to the Church out of fealty and because of benefices. Even the king himself often and persistently prohibited him from exercising canonical justice against his subjects, even when their crimes demanded it. Indeed, against property and persons, the lay authority appropriated all [cases] at will, with ecclesiastical law scorned, and with the bishops silent or muttering rather than resisting. The king attempted with promises and enticements to incline the archbishop to agree with him. But the man of God, solid and founded on a rock,[35] could not be softened by enticements or frightened by threats to deviate from the pursuit of justice.

13. And so, through malicious interpretation, wicked men tried to vilify this change in the right hand of the Most High[36] by ascribing to superstition the fact that he was leading a stricter life. They falsely asserted that his zeal for justice was cruelty. They attributed to avarice the fact that he procured advantages for the Church. They said that his contempt for worldly favor was the pursuit of glory, and the magnificence of his court was made out to be pride. That he followed a divinely instructed will in many situations was branded a mark of arrogance. That he often seemed to surpass the goals of his predecessors in defending justice was judged to be a sign of rashness. Indeed, nothing could now be said or done by him that the malice of unhappy men did not distort even to such an extent that they persuaded the king that if

32. This is another allusion to King Henry II's attempt to remove jurisdictional privileges of the clergy by reestablishing ancient, ancestral customs.

33. John 17.12.

34. Roger de Pont l'Évêque was appointed archbishop of York in 1154. He was hostile to Becket from their days together in Theobald's household, and remained his adversary throughout Becket's conflict with the king.

35. Matthew 7.25; Luke 6.48.

36. Psalm 76.11.

the archbishop's authority continued, without doubt the royal dignity would be destroyed; and unless the king looked out for himself and his heirs, a man would eventually become king whom the clergy would choose, and he would rule as long as he pleased the archbishop.

14. When the bishops and magnates convened at the king's command to settle necessary affairs of the realm,[37] it happened that a dispute arose between the king and the Church, which, protracted for a long time at the instigation of the devil, increased more and more each day. The bishops were all unanimously with their archbishop in his intention that they would most faithfully obey the king in those things which were of God, nor would they make any promise or enter into any obligation with him except as far as they could without violating their order. But it was brought about in many ways that the initial unity of the Church was split by certain bishops who seemed to be pillars of faith and religion,[38] so that either the archbishop might be corrupted with them or, if he stood alone, he might easily be worn down. Many were striving to trip up the man of God, but enemies in his household were distressing him most perniciously. The man of invincible constancy recalled that the person whom God stands by is not alone, and with Him as inspiration, he rose up secure from adversity, placing himself as a most solid wall before the house of Israel,[39] one who could not be broken by threats nor weakened by flattery. Indeed, he preferred to follow Christ the pauper as a pauper rather than to abandon the law of Christ, and with Christ comforting him, he was supported by a small number of paupers suffering with him.

15. When, after countless vexations and injuries, the bishops and magnates had at last convened at Clarendon [January 1164] at the royal command, the king very vehemently demanded that the customs of the realm,[40] which his grandfather seemed to have

37. The council assembled in October 1163 at Westminster Abbey in London.

38. During the fall of 1163, Gilbert Foliot and Hilary of Chichester joined Roger of York in withdrawing their support from Becket.

39. Ezechiel 13.5.

40. The king demanded observance of royal customs that he claimed were in force during the reign of his grandfather, Henry I. These included

observed with the approbation of the magnates, be publicly enum-
erated and confirmed by the clear and absolute assent of all the
bishops, with no conditions added at all. The attending archbishops and bishops tried as much as was allowed to block or at
least to defer this while they gauged the danger which inevitably
threatened from all directions. For if they should consent to vices
that had become habitual through wickedness, danger to the faith
and salvation followed without a doubt, but if they should resist,
the peace of the Church and safety of life was subject to certain
peril. And just cause for fear was not lacking, since according to
Solomon, "As the roaring of a lion, so is the wrath of a king."[41] The
weight of the war shifted to the archbishop. Without his counsel,
the counsel, as it were, of their own head, the bishops dared nothing, and they were afraid to advise him to acquiesce. He, however,
was more anxious about the dangers to certain bishops,[42] for
whom the loss of members [of their churches] and of their welfare
seemed imminent from the old hatred of the king, than he was
about his own perils, although many very severe ones threatened.
Ensnared as much by pressing need as by the persuasive words of
great men displaying the habit of religion, he gave his approval to
the king's demand as far as possible.[43] So both he and the bishops
for whom he feared escaped bodily danger, but with the loss of
their cause. The archbishop, fearing that in freeing their bodies [he
had brought] ruin on their souls, began to afflict himself harshly
by means of more austere foods and garments, and he suspended
himself from the office of the altar until he deserved to be forgiven,

---

jurisdiction in cases involving criminous clerks, relations with the pope, episcopal vacancies, and excommunications. In all, the Constitutions of Clarendon contained sixteen clauses.

41. Proverbs 19.12.

42. Here John likely refers to Jocelin of Salisbury and William of Nor-
wich, since both were already in disfavor with the king.

43. Henry had insisted that all bishops in the realm should assent to the
royal customs. Becket hesitated, but ultimately yielded and made a solemn
declaration that he would observe them.

absolved by the Roman pontiff through confession and proper
fruits of penance.[44]

16. The king's indignation did not cease, but through warnings
and terror he threatened more violence unless the customs which
he was striving to introduce in opposition to the Church were confirmed by the authority of the archbishops and bishops, and in
writing. Since Christ's confessor, the future martyr, dared to set
himself against the king's efforts, he was sometimes assailed with
many losses, provoked with insults and afflicted with injuries.
Finally [October 1164], dragged to Northampton under an unjust
law he endured patiently enough being convicted in a certain
money-related case, even though it was an unjust decision, and he
took care that the fine was sufficiently paid to the king. Then they
hurled other false accusations against him, though not at all summoned on that account, under the pretext of his giving a reckoning
of affairs entrusted to him at the time when he held the chancellorship. He was so harassed over these matters, in violation of
what was lawful and right, that it was necessary for him to appeal
to the apostolic see against the bishops, lest they should convict
him through an unjust judgment in order thus to please the king
and lest, in the same way, he be summoned by them to a hearing
before the lord pope.

17. Although the appeal against the magnates succeeded and
they were prohibited under a threat of excommunication from
bringing forward a verdict against their own father and judge, they
nevertheless presumed, as the pinnacle of their own damnation,
not so much to pronounce a verdict as to spew forth the madness
of the rage they had conceived against him, who had neither confessed nor been convicted, but who was merely bearing witness to
the Church's prerogative and his own, and invoking the support of
common law. When they wanted to make the verdict known in
public, the holy man, raising on high the cross of Christ which he
was holding in his hand and which he constantly carried about in

---

44. As soon as he departed from Clarendon, Becket repented of his
actions there and suspended himself from sacerdotal duties. Some biographers even declare that he resigned his archbishopric at a meeting with
Pope Alexander III in November 1164, but the pontiff restored it to him.

his heart and on his body, departed from that deadly court while the wicked ones cried out that he should be seized as a traitor and deservedly hanged. And so that the faithful servant might recognize as applicable to himself the glory of his Lord, almost on every side he heard, "Crucify him, crucify him!"[45] However, passing through their midst, he went away.[46]

18. When he had returned to his lodgings, two great and most faithful magnates approached him in the quiet of the night. They were pitiable in aspect and tearful, beating their breasts, confessing and bearing witness by the dreadful judgment of God that they knew without a doubt that powerful men, notorious for evil deeds, as one might expect of those defiled by many crimes, had plotted his murder and had bound each other by mutual oaths to kill him. Therefore, lest the cause of the Church, which had not yet become fully known, might suffer a setback by his death, the archbishop took flight on the same night, and with only one brother bringing him comfort, he hid by day and continued his journey at night. Sixteen days later he arrived at the harbor of Sandwich. And since there were no stronger conveyances at hand, he was ferried across to Flanders in a fragile little boat by two priests, with a few others hindering the navigation more than providing any solace or assistance.[47]

19. And so, driven into exile, the confessor of Christ was received with respect by the Lord Pope Alexander[48] at Sens and commended by him to the monastery at Pontigny.[49] But the king of the English dispatched his own bishops and magnates to the Roman Church, promising many things, provided that legates be sent who might, with all appeals removed, decide the case of the archbishop of Canterbury, which he demanded be settled immediately.

45. Mark 15.13–14.
46. Luke 4.30.
47. Becket sailed from Sandwich early in the morning on 2 November 1164 and reached Flanders on the same day.
48. Before his election to the papacy, Orlando (Roland) Bandinelli, a Sienese, was professor of law at Bologna. He served the Church as Pope Alexander III from September 1159–August 1181.
49. Becket took up residence at the Cistercian monastery at Pontigny late in 1164 and remained at this remote abbey in Burgundy until November 1166.

For it seemed to him that the cardinals could be persuaded and that a number of witnesses could very easily be procured on every point of the case. But, when he learned from his returning messengers that he had been refused in this request, the king ordered that the Church and all goods belonging to the archbishop and his men should be confiscated. And, what is unheard of anywhere in history, he sentenced to exile all the archbishop's kinsmen and all who were connected to him by friendship or any pretext at all, without distinction of rank or order, of status or fortune, of age or sex, for both women lying in childbirth and infants wailing in their cradles were driven into exile. His savage fury and cruelty, dreadful to the ears of the faithful, proceeded farther, for although the Catholic Church prays even for heretics and schismatics and faithless Jews, it was forbidden for anyone to assist the archbishop, even by the aid of prayers. Also, the ministers of public authority compelled all adults to swear that they would go to Pontigny for the sake of distressing him. There, in fact, the holy man tormented himself with long fasts and prayers, praying constantly for the Church, and for the king and the kingdom of the English, until the king took steps to drive him from there [Pontigny] by using the Cistercian abbots who had convened for a general chapter about their land [in England].[50] But before the archbishop left there, he was comforted by a divine revelation, a sign shown to him from heaven, that he would return with glory to his own Church and from there depart to the Lord with the palm of martyrdom. And just as the Blessed Virgin, whose soul a sword of sorrow pierced at the passion of her Son, is said to have lived as more than a martyr,[51] so also the confessor of Christ, while he endured many, great, long and unheard-of sufferings against himself and his people, gloriously showed forth the merit and the crown of martyrdom. But fearing that injury was threatening the holy men [there] on his account, he departed of his own will and

50. At a general council of the order held at Cîteaux in September 1166, Henry II threatened to expel the Cistercians from his realms if they did not remove Thomas Becket from Pontigny.

51. Saint Bernard of Clairvaux, "Sermon for the Sunday within the Octave of the Assumption," 14-15.

betook himself to Louis, the most-Christian king of the French,[52] who, receiving him with reverence, attended to his needs most humanely until peace should be restored. He also exhorted the supreme pontiff, by virtue of his love and under declaration of his devoted obedience, as [the pope] loved the kingdom of the French and the honor of the apostolic see, not to continue obstructive delays any longer. Also, having pity on the desolation of the English Church, the venerable bishop, William of Sens,[53] also entreated the apostolic see and obtained from the Roman Church [the following in early spring 1170]: that the king of the English should be excommunicated, with every appeal invalid, and the kingdom placed under interdict unless peace was restored to the Church at Canterbury.

20. Meanwhile, those who hated peace in the Church procured this: Roger, the archbishop of York, presumed to crown Henry, the king's son, in the province of Canterbury, after the prohibition of the lord pope and in opposition to the dignity of the Church of Canterbury and to ancient custom.[54] The suffragan bishops assisted him and did not declare in public the right of the Church of Canterbury. Thus, with injuries multiplied and perverse men ever-abusing the patience of Christ more and more, a multiple, certain and swift threat was issued against the king and his men. A day was set for decision so that sentence could not be deferred beyond it. Therefore, bound by the strictness of canon law, the king finally gave his assent that peace should be restored to the English Church.[55] And so the kingdom rejoiced, with everyone trusting that the matter was being carried out truthfully rather than conceived insincerely, but what was done by certain people, the outcome of the matter revealed. For Christ's bishop, judging others by his own good faith, was hoping for better things from those

---

52. Louis VII was king of France from 1137–1180. His relations with Henry II were tense, and he was generally supportive of Becket and his cause.

53. Known as William of the White Hands, this archbishop of Sens was a loyal supporter of Archbishop Becket.

54. Henry, "the Young King," was crowned by Roger of York at Westminster Abbey on 14 June 1170.

55. King Henry and Archbishop Becket reconciled their differences and restored their friendship at a meeting near Fréteval on 22 July 1170.

entering agreements with him. And although many advised him
not to dare to return unless peace were more surely confirmed,
yet, fearing the peril of souls, he returned in the seventh year of
exile to his own Church.⁵⁶ The king offered him safe-conduct, and
he was received by the clergy and the people as if he were an angel
of the Lord.⁵⁷

21. But when the lord pope heard, through the complaint of
Saint Thomas, about the aforementioned presumption of the
already-named archbishop of York and the bishops who assisted
him [at the coronation], he suspended the archbishop of York and
the bishops supporting him from their episcopal office, and he
renewed his sentence of excommunication against Gilbert of London and Jocelin of Salisbury.⁵⁸ This severity, made public upon
Saint Thomas's arrival, angered the king even more and rendered
the poisoned tongues of his detractors more efficacious for doing
harm. Therefore, Christ's champion was afflicted again by losses,
again by more atrocious injuries beyond measure and number,
and by public decree he was prevented from leaving the enclosure
of his own church. Whoever showed him or any of his men a
cheerful countenance was considered a public enemy. But the man
of God suffered all these things with much patience, preferring to
endure not only the loss of possessions but also of safety rather
than to endanger the justice of God and the liberty of the Church
without rendering aid or without at least crying out in protest.
With all due respect to all the saints, I say: if anyone sacrifices as
much to God as he forsakes for love of Him, no one is easily found
who would surpass Thomas. Certainly, for Christ he considered his
own possessions and people, he considered the world, he even
considered himself as of no importance.

22. And since my pen hastens toward the confessor's passion,
the authors and cause of which are well known from many power-

56. Becket arrived in England on 1 December 1170 after six years in exile.
57. In a letter (no. 304) to Peter, abbot of Saint Rémi (Rheims), John of
Salisbury described his own reception by the clergy and people at Canterbury
in these same terms.
58. The pope had excommunicated these bishops in September 1170.
Gilbert Foliot was bishop of London from 1163–1187; Jocelin was bishop of
Salisbury from 1142–1184. Both were adversaries of Becket.

ful proofs, I have decided not to dwell longer on this, especially since the matter is known and has been spread abroad almost throughout the Latin world by the reports of many. Yet I do not believe that I should be silent about so great a gift of the divine dispensation as this, which all marvel at to the glory of God and His martyr, since all the circumstances so come together in the archbishop's struggle that they forever illustrate the glory of his suffering, and they reveal the impiety of his persecutors and stain their name for all time with shame. Indeed, if it is pleasing to consider and to take the measure of the persons on this side and that, there appears on this side the archbishop, a man of religion, primate of Britain, legate of the apostolic see, a most incorrupt judge, inasmuch as he was one who accepts neither persons nor bribes, a champion of ecclesiastical freedom, and, as it were, a lofty tower in Jerusalem against the face of Damascus,[59] a hammer of the impious, but a consoler of the poor and grieving. Let him who wishes see who comes forward from the opposite side. And if the cause makes the martyr,[60] which no right-thinking person doubts, what cause was more just, more holy than his? He rejected riches and every glory of the world, the affection of friends and of all his relatives for love of Christ; he endured exile and exposed himself and all his men to perils and poverty. He fought even unto death to defend the law of his God and to cancel the abuses of ancient tyrants. And after he fell once, caught by the guile of those lying in ambush, in no other obligation could he be induced to promise any of those things which were demanded of him without adding that in all matters the honor of God and the integrity of the Church would be preserved. He did not suffer adversities, believing for a little while, for an hour, as it were, and falling away in a moment of temptation, but he prolonged his exile and bitter proscription to the seventh year, walking the royal way[61] and following the footsteps of Christ and the Apostles with so great a virtue of constancy that his unconquered spirit could not be broken by the force of cruel fortune nor weakened by blandishments. But also, look

59. Cf. Song of Solomon 7.4.
60. Augustine, Sermon 275.
61. Numbers 21.22.

where he was sacrificed! In the Church which is the head of the realm and the mother of all others in Christ, before the altar, among fellow-priests and a band of monks whom the uproar of armed murderers caused to run toward an astonishing and deplorable spectacle. And so, the one who had for a long time shown himself to be a living victim, holy and pleasing to God;[62] who had crucified his flesh, along with its vices and desires,[63] in prayers and vigils, fasts and the use of a rough hair shirt; who was accustomed, like a child of Christ, to expose his back to whips (which only his close followers knew); who was wont to offer Christ's body and blood on the altar, offered his own blood, shed by the hands of impious men as he lay prostrate before the altar.

23. And what their predecessors allowed in the crucifixion of the Master and Lord, these accomplices of Satan did not allow in the sacrificing of His disciple and servant. For lest the city be defiled, lest the sabbath be polluted, Christ was led out of the city. Even though He had been condemned at an unjust trial, He had received an opportunity, such as it was, to argue on His own behalf. He was crucified beyond the gate, certainly with the help of gentiles who did not know God, and by the authority of the public power, accused by those whose law He seemed to impugn, and with His own disciple, a son of perdition,[64] seeing to the treachery of His betrayal. But the archbishop [was murdered] not only in the city, but within his church; not at an ordinary time, but on a day which the celebration of the Lord's birth made holy. And by every right it was fitting that the feast day of him who had lived innocently and most purely should follow the feast of the Holy Innocents. Indeed, it is believed, his disciples, traitors, procured his death, and the chief priests planned it. The more diligently they took precautions lest he be brought to trial; lest he be confronted by his accusers; lest he appear before the face of a judge; lest through the privilege of a holy place or time, or office or rank, or on the grounds that peace had been restored and security granted, he escape the sacrilegious hands, not of pagans, not of enemies,

62. Romans 12.1.
63. Galatians 5.24.
64. John 17.12.

but of those who professed the law of God and the fidelity of friends, the more they surpassed Annas and Caiphas, Pilate and Herod in malice. Truly, it happened through the wondrous working of God, Who regulates all things wisely and advantageously, that He, Who allowed these things to be done so wickedly, so unwisely and shamelessly, did not suffer them to be concealed, so that here also in time might be fulfilled that which Truth proclaimed: "Nothing is hidden which will not be revealed."[65] For what has been made known through frequent telling about Judas, the standard-bearer of betrayers, by equal right must be attributed to his accomplices because it is evident that the judgment is the same concerning similar matters, so that it is clear to all Christians in good faith that the heavens will reveal these men's iniquity and the earth will rise up against them.[66] Who among the faithful would dare to doubt that God will either convert or crush the authors and perpetrators of so great a sacrilege?

24. As he was about to suffer before the altar in the church, as was said, Christ's martyr, before he was struck, heard that he was being sought by knights who had come for this purpose and were crying out amidst the crowd standing around, "Where is the archbishop?" He replied to them from the stairs, which he had partly ascended, saying with an undaunted expression on his face, "Here I am; what do you want?" Then one of the murderous knights said to him in a spirit of rage, "That you die now, for it is impossible that you should live longer." But the archbishop responded with no less constancy of speech than of spirit (since, with all due respect to all the martyrs, I would confidently say to the best of my knowledge and belief, no one seems to have been more constant than he): "Indeed, I am prepared to die for my God and for the assertion of justice and liberty for the Church. But if you seek my life, on behalf of Almighty God and under pain of excommunication I forbid you to harm anyone else in any way, whether monk or cleric or layman, greater or lesser, but let them be exempt from the punishment just as they are from its cause. Not to them but to me must it be imputed if any of them has taken up the cause

65. Matthew 10.26.
66. Job 20.27.

of the struggling Church. I willingly embrace death, provided that in the pouring out of my blood the Church secures peace and liberty." Who is seen to be more fervent in love than this man, who, when he offered himself to his persecutors for the sake of God's law, was concerned for this alone: that those nearest him not be injured in any way? Do his words not seem to imitate Christ, who said at His Passion, "If you seek me, let these go."[67]

25. After these words were spoken, seeing the assassins with drawn swords, he inclined his head forward in the manner of one praying and said these very last words: "To God and Blessed Mary, and the patron saints of this church, and to Saint Denys, I commend myself and the cause of the Church."

26. Who could relate the rest without sighs, gasps and tears? Piety does not permit me to describe the individual crimes which those savage murderers committed, scorning the fear of God and unmindful of their faith as well as of all humanity. Indeed, it was not enough for them to desecrate the church with the blood and murder of a priest, and to defile a most holy day, but when the crown of his head had been cut off (which anointing with holy chrism had consecrated to God), they also – horrible to say! – thrust out the brains of the now-deceased man with their deadly swords and most cruelly scattered them, along with his blood and bones, on the pavement. They were more monstrous than the crucifiers of Christ, who did not think that the legs of one whom they saw was dead should be broken, as they did to those still living. Amidst all these torments the martyr of unconquered spirit and admirable constancy did not utter a word or cry, he did not emit a groan, he did not hold out his arm or his clothing to [fend off] the one striking him, but he held his head, which he exposed in a bowed position to the swords, immobile until the deed was finished. Then falling forward to the ground with his body straight, he did not move a foot or hand, while the assassins were insolently declaring that, in the slaughter of a traitor, they had restored peace to the country. No less greedy than cruel, the murderers went back to the palace belonging to the church and in an affront to the royal authority as well as to the divine majesty, with insatiable avarice

67. John 18.8.

and astonishing boldness, they plundered all the furnishings and whatever could be found in the boxes and saddle-bags of the archbishop and his men, be it gold or silver or clothes or various ornaments or books or charters or all other writings, or horse-trappings. They divided these among themselves as they pleased, made imitators of those who distributed Christ's garments among themselves, although in a certain way they surpassed them in wickedness. And in order that men's favor might be taken away from the archbishop now crowned through martyrdom, all the written materials which the sacrilegious plunderers stole were sent to the king in Normandy. But by divine will it came to pass that the more human rashness strove to obscure the glory of His bravest champion, so much the more did the Lord illuminate it in the display of his virtue and the manifest proofs of miracles. Seeing this, the impious men who hated him insatiably, in the name of public authority prevented anyone from presuming to proclaim openly the miracles which were happening. But one desires in vain to darken what God decides to make bright, for the more zealously the miracles seemed to those impious ones to be concealed the more prevalent they became. Man sees the face; it is God alone, Who searches loins and hearts.[68] For when the blessed martyr's body was given up for burial and clothed according to custom in episcopal vestments, it was found to be wrapped in a hair shirt full of lice and worms, a fact which very few of his closest friends had known; also, hidden thigh-coverings made of hair and extending to his knees were found, something which had not been heard of before among our people.

27. Who could hear or tell what follows without weeping? The church that had been profaned, or rather consecrated, by holy blood dared to suspend itself from divine services to protest the injury to God, yet not without hesitation and much deliberation out of fear of impious men. But so great a terror from evident signs assailed the provincial bishops that there was no one at all, or very rarely one, who dared to cease from divine services as a display of justice, or to solemnly offer the final rites owed the dead in Christ as the duty of humanity. Impious men were doing this so that his

68. Psalm 7.10.

name might be blotted out forever. In all these things the fury of his persecutors did not rest; they said that the body of a traitor must not be buried among holy bishops, but cast into a vile swamp or suspended on a gibbet. Thus, before the servants of Satan who had been summoned to perpetrate these sacrileges might assemble, the holy men who were present, fearing that force would be brought against them, buried him in a marble coffin in the crypt in front of the altar of Saint John the Baptist and Saint Augustine, the apostle of the English.

28. There, to the glory of Almighty God, many mighty miracles have happened in this place. People flock there in crowds to see in others and sense in themselves the power and mercy of Him Who is always wondrous and glorious in His saints. For in the place of his suffering, and in the spot before the high altar where he passed the night before being interred, and where he finally was buried, paralytics are cured, the blind see, the deaf hear, mutes speak, the lame walk, lepers are cleansed,[69] those with fevers recover, those possessed by a demon are set free, and those sick with various diseases are cured; blasphemers possessed by a demon are confounded and, what has not been heard of from the days of our fathers, the dead rise. These and more miracles, which it is a long task to tell, God works, Who alone is blessed beyond all things forever. Amen.

HERE ENDS THE LIFE OF BLESSED THOMAS THE MARTYR.

---

69. This passage echoes Matthew 11.5 and Luke 7.22.

Selected Bibliography

1. EDITIONS AND TRANSLATIONS

EADMER

Ed. and trans. R.W. Southern. *The Life of St. Anselm, Archbishop of Canterbury*. Oxford: Clarendon Press, 1972 [c1962].

JOHN OF SALISBURY

ENTHETICUS

Trans. Ronald E. Pepin. "John of Salisbury's Entheticus." *Allegorica* 9 (1987–1988) 7–133.

Ed. and trans. Jan van Laarhoven. *John of Salisbury's Entheticus Maior and Minor*. 3 vols. Studien und Texte zur Geistesgeschichte des Mittelalters 17. Leiden/New York: Brill, 1987.

HISTORIA PONTIFICALIS

Ed. and trans. Marjorie Chibnall. *The Historia pontificalis of John of Salisbury*. Oxford Medieval Texts. Rpt. Oxford: Clarendon Press, 1986 [c1965].

LETTERS

Ed. and trans. W.J. Millor and H.E. Butler, rev. by C.N.L. Brooke. *The Letters of John of Salisbury*. Vol. 1 (The Early Letters). Oxford: Clarendon Press, 1986 [c1955].

Ed. and trans. W.J. Millor and C.N.L. Brooke. *The Letters of John of Salisbury*. Vol. 2 (The Later Letters). Oxford: Clarendon Press, 1979.

METALOGICON

Trans. Daniel D. McGarry. *The Metalogicon of John of Salisbury: A Twelfth-Century Defense of the Verbal and Logical Arts of the Trivium*. Rpt. Westport, CN: Greenwood Press, 1982 [c1955].

POLICRATICUS

Trans. John Dickinson. *The Statesman's Book, Being the Fourth, Fifth and Sixth Books, and Selections from the Seventh and Eighth Books of the Policraticus.* New York: Russell & Russell, 1963 [c1927].

Trans. Murray F. Markland. *Policraticus: The Statesman's Book* [selections]. Milestones of Thought in the History of Ideas. New York: Frederick Ungar, 1979.

Trans. Cary J. Nederman. *Policraticus: Of the Frivolities of Courtiers and the Footprints of Philosophers* [selections]. Cambridge Texts in the History of Political Thought. Rev. ed. Cambridge: Cambridge University Press, 1996 [1990].

Trans. Joseph B. Pike. *Frivolities of Courtiers and Footprints of Philosophers, Being a Translation of the First, Second, and Third Books, and Selections from the Seventh and Eighth Books of the Policraticus.* Rpt. New York: Octagon Books, 1972 [c1938].

LIVES OF ANSELM AND BECKET

Ed. and trans. [Italian] Inos Biffi. *Vita di sant'Anselmo d'Aosta.* Milan: Jaca Books, 1988.

Ed. Inos Biffi. *Anselmo e Becket, Due Vite.* Milan: Jaca Book Ed., 1990.

Ed. J.C. Robertson. "Vita Sancti Thomae Cantuariensis Archiepiscopi et Martyris." In *Materials for the History of Thomas Becket.* Rolls Series 67 (1875–1885) 2: 301–322.

Ed. D.J. Sheerin. "An Anonymous Verse Epitome of the Life of St. Anselm." *Analecta Bollandiana* 92 (1974) 109–124.

2. SECONDARY SOURCES

Barker, Lynn K. "MS Bodl. Canon. Pat. Lat. 131 and a Lost Lactantius of John of Salisbury: Evidence in Search of a French Critic of Thomas Becket." *Albion* 22 (1990) 21–37.

Barlow, Frank. *Thomas Becket.* Berkeley: University of California Press, 1986.

_____. "John of Salisbury and His Brothers." *Journal of Ecclesiastical History* 46 (1995) 95–109.

Brooke, Christopher Nugent Lawrence. "Adrian IV and John of Salisbury." In *Adrian IV, The English Pope (1154–1159): Studies and Texts*, ed. Brenda Bolton and Anne J. Duggan, 3–13. Aldershot: Ashgate, 2003.

Constable, Giles. "The Alleged Disgrace of John of Salisbury in 1159." *English Historical Review* 69 (1954) 67–76.

Duggan, Anne J. "John of Salisbury and Thomas Becket." In *The World of John of Salisbury*, ed. Michael Wilks, 427–438. Oxford: Basil Blackwell, 1984.

_____. *Thomas Becket*. London: Arnold; New York: Oxford University Press, 2004.

_____. *Thomas Becket: Friends, Networks, Texts and Cult*. Aldershot: Ashgate, 2007.

Hall, J.B. "Notes on the 'Entheticus' of John of Salisbury." *Traditio* 39 (1983) 444–447.

Hirata, Yoko. "John of Salisbury and Thomas Becket: The Making of a Martyr." *Medieval History* 2 (1992) 18–25.

Jackson, W.T.H. *Medieval Literature: A History and a Guide*. New York: Collier, 1966.

Jeauneau, Edouard. "'Nani gigantum humeris insidentes': Essai d'interprétation de Bernard de Chartres." *Vivarium* 5 (1967) 77–99.

Keats-Rohan, K.S.B. "John of Salisbury and Education in Twelfth-Century Paris from the Account of His *Metalogicon*." *History of Universities* 6 (1986) 1–45.

_____. "The Chronology of John of Salisbury's Studies in France: A Reading of 'Metalogicon' II.10." *Studi Medievali*, 3rd series, 28 (1987) 193–203.

Knowles, David. *The Evolution of Medieval Thought*. Baltimore: Vintage, 1962.

_____. *Thomas Becket*. Stanford: Stanford University Press, 1971.

Lépinois, E. de et Lucien Merlet. "Necrologium Ecclesiae Beatae Mariae Carnotensis." *Cartulaire de Notre-Dame de Chartres* (Chartres, 1862–1865) 3: 202.

Liebeschütz, Hans. *Medieval Humanism in the Life and Writings of John of Salisbury*. Studies of the Warburg Institute 17. London: The Warburg Institute, 1950.

Lounsbury, Richard. C. "The Case of the Erudite Eyewitness: Cicero, Lucan, and John of Salisbury." *Allegorica* 11 (1990) 15–35.

Martin, Janet. *John of Salisbury and the Classics*. Ph.D. dissertation, Harvard University, 1968.

———. "John of Salisbury as Classical Scholar." In *The World of John of Salisbury*, ed. Wilks, 179–201.

McLoughlin, John. "The Language of Persecution: John of Salisbury and the Early Phase of the Becket Dispute (1163–1166)." In *Persecution and Toleration: Papers Read at the Twenty-second Summer Meeting and the Twenty-third Winter Meeting of the Ecclesiastical History Society*, ed. William J. Sheils, 73–87. Studies in Church History 21. [Oxford]: Basil Blackwell, 1984.

———. "*Amicitia* in Practice: John of Salisbury (c.1120–1180) and His Circle." In *England in the Twelfth Century: Proceedings of the 1988 Harlaxton Symposium*, ed. Daniel Williams, 165–181. Woodbridge: Boydell & Brewer, 1990.

Merton, Robert K. *On the Shoulders of Giants: A Shandean Postscript*. New York: Harcourt, Brace & World, 1965.

Nadeau, Alain. "Notes on the Significance of John of Salisbury's 'Vita Anselmi.'" In *Twenty-Five Years (1969–1994) of Anselm Studies: Review and Critique of Recent Scholarly Views*, ed. Frederick Van Fleteren and Joseph C. Schnaubelt, 67–77. Texts and Studies in Religion 70; Anselm Studies 3. Lewiston, NY: Edwin Mellen Press, 1996.

Nederman, Cary J. *John of Salisbury*. Medieval and Renaissance Texts and Studies 288. Tempe: Arizona Center for Medieval and Renaissance Studies, 2005.

———. "A Duty to Kill: John of Salisbury's Theory of Tyrannicide." *The Review of Politics* 50 (1988) 365–389.

———. "The Changing Face of Tyranny: The Reign of King Stephen in John of Salisbury's Political Thought." *Nottingham Medieval Studies* 33 (1989) 1–20.

———, and Catherine Campbell. "Priests, Kings, and Tyrants: Spiritual and Temporal Power in John of Salisbury's *Policraticus*." *Speculum* 66 (1991) 572–590.

_____, and Arlene Feldwick. "To the Court and Back Again: The Origins and Dating of the *Entheticus de Dogmate Philosophorum* of John of Salisbury." *Journal of Medieval and Renaissance Studies* 21 (1991) 129–145.

Newman, John Henry. *Apologia pro vita sua*. Ed. David J. DeLaura. New York: W.W. Norton, 1968.

Newman, Jonathan M. "Satire between School and Court: The Ethical Interpretation of the *Artes* in John of Salisbury's *Entheticus in dogmata philosophorum*." *The Journal of Medieval Latin* 17 (2007) 125-142.

Pepin, Ronald E. "'On the Conspiracy of the Members,' Attributed to John of Salisbury." *Allegorica* 12 (1991) 29–41.

_____. *"Amicitia Jocosa:* Peter of Celle and John of Salisbury." *Florilegium* 5 (1983) 140–156.

_____. "John of Salisbury's *Entheticus* and the Classical Tradition of Satire." *Florilegium* 3 (1981) 215–227.

_____. "Fulgentius – The Enigmatic *Furvus* in John of Salisbury's 'Entheticus.'" *Mittellateinisches Jahrbuch* 23 (1988) 119–125.

Ray, Roger. "Rhetorical Scepticism and Verisimilar Narrative in John of Salisbury's *Historia Pontificalis*." In *Classical Rhetoric and Medieval Historiography*, ed. Ernst Breisach, 61–102. Studies in Medieval Culture 19. Kalamazoo, MI: Medieval Institute Publications, 1985.

Rouse, Richard H. and Mary A. Rouse. "John of Salisbury and the Doctrine of Tyrannicide." *Speculum* 42 (1967) 693–707.

Staunton, Michael. *The Lives of Thomas Becket*. Manchester Medieval Sources Series. Manchester and New York: Manchester University Press, 2001.

_____. *Thomas Becket and His Biographers*. Studies in the History of Medieval Religion 28. Woodbridge: The Boydell Press, 2006.

Southern, R.W. *Saint Anselm and His Biographer: A Study of Monastic Life and Thought, 1059–c.1130*. Cambridge: Cambridge University Press, 1963.

Stock, Brian. "Antiqui and Moderni as 'Giants' and 'Dwarfs': A Reflection of Popular Culture?" *Modern Philology* 76 (1979) 370–374.

Thomson, Rodney. "What Is the Entheticus?" In *The World of John of Salisbury*, ed. Michael Wilks, 287–301.

van Laarhoven, Jan. "Thou Shall *Not* Slay a Tyrant! The So-called Theory of John of Salisbury." In *The World of John of Salisbury*, ed. Wilks, 319–341.

Wilks, Michael J., ed. *The World of John of Salisbury*. Studies in Church History, Subsidia 3. Oxford: Basil Blackwell, 1984.

Index